Advance praise for *Raising Passionate Readers*

"Raising Passionate Readers is a perfect primer for parents looking to instill a love of reading in children. I regularly share Nancy Newman's advice with families at my library and use her techniques with my own children."
— Carrie Silberman M.L.S., Head of Children's Library,
New York Society Library

"Nancy Newman delineates clear, simple, and powerful steps that promote a love of reading, one of the essential foundations for success in school and in life."
— Jonathan Cohen, Ph.D., A.B.P.P., President, National School
Climate Center; author, *Educating Minds and Hearts*

"Raising Passionate Readers is rich with ideas for having fun while sharing adventures in language. Any parent, grandparent, or educator can benefit from this book!"
— Emily Comstock Di Martino, Ph.D., specialist in children's literature,
Director of Teacher Education, Baruch College, City
University of New York

"Follow Nancy Newman's wise, joyous advice and your child won't lift his eyes from his favorite book!"
— Patricia Laurence, Ph.D., City University of New York

"Raising Passionate Readers is a deeply valuable book that reminds us of the importance of reading in a fast-paced, technological world."
— Marlene Velo, Executive Director, KIDS Research Center

Acclaim for Nancy Newman

"Inspirational and encouraging advice on how to make reading and learning fun without the urgency of a hurried performance."
— Rosemary Milliman, Principal of Lower School, Trinity School

"The school was buzzing with enthusiasm for your presentation which balanced the reality of parenting with practical tips every parent felt they could manage at home. Your message was clear, simple, and encouraging."
— Nancy Schulman, former Director, 92nd St. Y Nursery School; Division Head: Early Learning Center, Avenues School

"You speak to parents from the perspective of one who has been in their shoes and survived to tell about it! Your suggestions are such simple, practical things that one doesn't often think of but yet are so easy to do."
— Deborah Markewich, Parent Coordinator, Public School 166

"More parents raved to me about your workshop than any workshop we have had. It was really inspirational."
— Lydia Spinelli, Director, Brick Church School

"Your creative ideas can be implemented stress free. Parents, teachers, college professors, and learning specialists all walked away with valuable information."
— Linda Selvin, former Executive Director, New York Branch of the International Dyslexia Association

Raising Passionate Readers

Raising Passionate Readers

5 Easy Steps to Success in School and Life

Nancy Newman

TRIBECA VIEW PRESS

New York

TRIBECA VIEW PRESS 2014

Copyright © 2014 by Nancy Newman
41 River Terrace
New York, New York 10282

Publisher's Cataloging-In-Publication Data

Newman, Nancy, 1944 –
  Raising passionate readers: 5 easy steps to success in school and life / Nancy Newman.
  — 1st ed.

  p. : ill. ; cm.

  Includes bibliographical references and index.
  ISBN: 978-0-615-84754-2

  1. Reading—Parent participation. 2. Children—Books and reading. I. Title.

LB1139.5.R43 N49 2014
649.58   2013951969

This book is available at special discounts for bulk purchases in the U.S. by corporations, institutions, and other organizations. For more information, please contact the Special Markets Department at Tribeca View Press by emailing info@tribecaviewpress.com.

Designed by Régis Zaleman

FIRST EDITION

ISBN 978-0-615-84754-2

Printed and bound in the United States of America

For my husband, H.H.E., with love.

Contents

Part 1   **Background Information**

Introduction   *Who I Am and Why I've Written This Book* 15

Chapter 1   *Power to the Parents!* 25

Chapter 2   *Ignore the Myths About Reading!* 31

Part 2   **The Five Steps**

Chapter 3   *Step One:* 45

Talk, Talk, Talk to Your Infant, Toddler, and School-Age Child

Chapter 4   *Step Two:* 67

Encourage Free Play and Fiercely Protect Free Time

Chapter 5   *Step Three:* 85

Read to Your Child and Expand How, When, and What You Read Aloud

Chapter 6   *Step Four:* 113

Support and Motivate Your New Reader

Chapter 7   *Step Four ... continued:* 139

Give Extra Support to Your Struggling Reader

Chapter 8   *Step Five* 159

Use—Don't Abuse—Technology and Balance Your Child's Diet of Fun

Chapter 9   *A Final Word on a*
               Passion for Reading...179

Notes 181

Acknowledgments 198

Bibliography...200

Index..217

Part 1

Background Information

Introduction

Who I Am and Why I've Written This Book

Flames shot up from the garbage pail as students hooted and tossed paper balls into the blaze. I shouted for help and a janitor rushed in with a fire extinguisher. Foam smothered the flames, but I was left in despair. My high school English classes were so chaotic, I felt I was more policeman than teacher. Most of my sixteen-year-old students could barely read—and I didn't know how to help them.

The year was 1965. I was a newly minted New York City public school teacher in my early twenties. I was idealistic and determined to make a difference in young people's lives. But I was confronting a seemingly insurmountable barrier that stumped me—and many of my colleagues.

Some days, as I gazed into the angry, sullen faces of my teenage students, I searched for traces of the sparkly-eyed six-year-olds they must have been in kindergarten. Every little child I'd ever met loved books and couldn't wait to learn to read. Why did these kids lose their passion for books and their excitement about learning? What happened to their appetite for reading and their explosive intellectual energy?

These questions echoed through my mind as I struggled week in and week out to reignite my students' interest in reading. But I couldn't get past their indifference—if not downright hostility. Eventually, I slunk out of that inner-city high school and took a job as a remedial writing instructor at a community college in one of the surrounding boroughs.

Now that I didn't have to deal with discipline problems, I expected to be a more effective teacher. But my college students' glazed-over expressions, loud and frequent yawns, and carelessly written papers soon told me that I wasn't getting through to them either. For the next three semesters I tried everything I could think of, short of setting off fireworks in class, to trigger an interest in the reading assignments I handed out. Nothing seemed to work. My students were taking the class to fulfill a requirement and had zero interest in improving their language skills. They just wanted to pass.

Then, toward the end of my third semester at the college, I had an *aha!* moment and figured it out. Students disliked books because written language was a source of frustration rather than a helpful tool. The only way I could give them the skills they needed was to change the way they *felt* about reading and writing. They needed to see that words could be fun.

Eager to try out a radical new approach, I left the college English department to help a group of equally frustrated teachers establish an experimental program for "underachievers" on campus. Classes would be held in trailers that had been towed into the parking lot for our use; students would be a mix of eighteen-year-olds who were about to flunk out of college, ex-convicts from a local halfway house, and Vietnam vets who wanted to take another stab at school.

On a sunny fall morning, students shuffled into the trailer for our first class and sat down nervously. I introduced myself by my first name, announced that I was terminating the traditional teacher/student contract (I'll pretend to teach, you'll pretend to learn), and said that I wouldn't assign written work until we *talked* about writing in class. Then I asked the students to tell me why they were attending college.

Suspicious of my unconventional introduction, not to mention my long braids, fringed cowgirl skirt, and tie-dyed shirt (remember, it was the sixties), one by one, class members fed me what they thought an English teacher would want to hear. But I wouldn't let them off the hook and kept pressing for more honesty, teasing and joking and talking so openly about my life that they slowly opened up. When a burly Vietnam vet in his early thirties admitted he'd always despised English classes, his honesty jolted the group into silence. Then a meek-looking woman in the back of the trailer said, *"I've always hated English teachers,"* and everyone twisted in their seats to study her. Suddenly, people began swapping horror stories about teachers and school, their tales of failure and embarrassment dating all the way back to first grade.

Astonished by the outpouring of anguish I heard that day, I realized that despite vast differences in their age, race, ethnicity, income, and background, most of my students had one thing in common: early reading problems. Their inability to learn to read well in grade school had mangled their self-esteem, destroyed their appetite for books, crippled them academically, and taken a heavy toll on other areas of their lives. As one student put it, *"I thought I was too dumb to learn to read, so books became enemies. I felt like a failure in school and quit as soon as I could—something I've been paying for ever since."*

I shared with the students my insights about written language as a source of frustration and began exploring why they might have had trouble learning to read. Did their parents speak standard English, a dialect of English, or a foreign language at home? Had the students received remedial help from a trained reading specialist? Had anyone encouraged them to practice reading? Did they have books and magazines in their homes? Had other members of their families struggled with reading? Had they been taken to the library as children? Gradually, as the students began to realize that their reading problems hadn't stemmed from their lack of intelligence but, rather, from a combination of other factors, they began to come alive in class. It was as if I'd flipped a switch in their brains; they became almost intoxicated by their ability to express their thoughts in a classroom setting.

I had discovered the first piece of the puzzle: Anxiety about reading problems that began in the early grades had caused my students to turn themselves off to books and to tune out in school. Now that they felt more comfortable in the classroom, they dropped their defenses and engaged in class discussions.

Soon, we began having freewheeling, heated, sometimes raucous exchanges and debates about the social and economic benefits of mastering standard English, and the relationships between language and thought, language and personal identity, language and social class, language and race, and language and power.

"Hey, why didn't anyone ever tell me reading and writing are about thinking, and thinking is fun?" a student blurted out one day.

That comment led me to another important insight: When children enter first grade, they associate books and reading with pleasure. But learning to read is such a long, slow, difficult process that they begin to associate reading with hard work and homework, and forget that books are a source of entertainment. In an effort to reverse this dynamic, I read aloud at the beginning of every class, choosing poems or short passages from novels that were by turns gripping, infuriating, witty, heart-stopping, or hilarious.

Then I asked students to write. *"Don't worry about the mechanics of writing,"* I told them. *"Just try to make your heart throb on paper."* Now that they began to see language as a tool rather than an enemy, they put genuine effort into assignments—and for the first time in their lives, they tasted the joys of focused self-expression. Once they wanted to communicate their thoughts and feelings on paper, I could help them tackle the grammar and punctuation problems that had crippled them in school.

I continued to fine-tune this approach during subsequent semesters, but my basic method remained the same: I reduced my students' anxiety about reading and writing and bolstered their self-confidence in the classroom so they would become fully engaged in the work. Then I rekindled their enjoyment of words and books by reading terrific material out loud and encouraging them to have fun expressing themselves on paper. After they were motivated to improve, I helped them spruce up their weak language skills.

I was hugely energized by this teaching experience. I had witnessed firsthand the transformation of people who had started out as defensive, bored, hostile students and had become enthusiastic learners who understood that language skills bring pleasure and power.

Fast-forward to the 1970s when I became a mother. I knew almost nothing about babies, but I was determined to protect my son from the reading problems that had plagued my former students, especially because dyslexia runs in our family. Despite my lack of experience with infants, I was confident I could pull this off because of two things I did know about children:

1 *Babies instinctively use language (or the sounds of language) for fun and have an almost insatiable appetite for learning—they play to learn and learn by playing.*

2 *Reading is hard work for beginners and only becomes enjoyable once children master the basics and become skilled experts who can read effortlessly.*

So my twin goal was to reinforce my son's natural enjoyment of language and learning, and—once he started school—to help him practice enough to become an effortless reader.

With these goals in the back of my mind (plus a desire to keep myself entertained), I informally adapted my classroom approach for home use, which basically meant doing a few simple things as I went about my normal, everyday life. First, I looked for opportunities to use words as toys by chatting, clowning around, singing, reading aloud, and making up silly rhymes and poems. I cultivated my son's desire for learning by encouraging him to play in and explore his environment. After he started school, I stoked his enthusiasm for books by continuing to read aloud, and I made it as easy and comfortable as possible for him to practice reading. Last, I protected him from overdosing on TV and computers so he would hold onto his habit of plugging into both books and technology for entertainment.

When my next two sons were born, I did these same five things from the time they were infants. The result? Although the two younger boys found reading a struggle and lagged behind classmates through much of grade school, all three boys became voracious readers and dazzling students.

"What are you doing with your kids?" other parents would invariably ask when they noticed that my sons loved to read.

"Uh, we're having a party," I'd answer without much thought.

"No, really, Nancy. What's your secret?"

My secret was that I had consciously shared the pleasure of words with my sons. But whenever I said this to people, they were skeptical.

"You can't get kids to read nowadays," they would say. *"Books can't compete with technology."*

Wherever I turned, someone was always insisting it was *"impossible"* to raise readers.

I knew differently. But because my approach came from my

own experience as a teacher and mother, I had no objective proof or validation that my method worked.

It turns out that while I had been searching for answers about children and reading on my own, a group of neuroscientists academics, psychologists, biologists, and learning specialists had been analyzing reading behavior in classrooms and laboratories across the country. In the 1980s, newly invented medical imaging tools such as computed tomography (CT) and functional magnetic resonance imaging (fMRI) enabled neuroscientists to study brain activity and find out exactly how children learn to read. This information allowed researchers to pinpoint the simple steps busy parents can take to help children become readers.

Yet here we are, three decades after scientists illuminated the reading process, and most people are still in the dark about reading. Chilling national statistics say it all: The National Assessment of Educational Progress reports that 37 percent of fourth graders have below basic reading skills—and the amount of reading failure is even higher within ethnic minority groups, low-income families, and English-language learners. The National Right to Read Foundation tells us that approximately 20 percent of all graduating high school seniors can be classified as functionally illiterate. And according to the National Endowment for the Arts, of the seventeen-year-olds who can read proficiently, only about 20 percent say they read anything for pleasure on a regular basis, including newspapers, magazines, and comic books.

All told, children's illiteracy (their inability to read) and aliteracy (their lack of desire to read) are wreaking havoc on the lives of individual children and our whole society.

I have written this book to share with other parents what researchers have discovered and what I have learned about children and reading. I believe that helping a child become a passionate reader enriches him socially, emotionally, and intellectually. It allows him to succeed in school and life, and enlarges his future. It is a gift that lasts a lifetime.

Chapter 1

Power to the Parents!

Your child's reading ability will seal his fate in school and affect just about every aspect of his life—his intelligence, self-confidence, relationships, career path, economic level, social status, level of inner satisfaction, and health.

It is no exaggeration to say reading will shape your child's future.

Now for the good news. It's easier to raise a skilled, enthusiastic reader than you might realize — and you can get started today.

- Even if you're busy.

- Even if your child is an infant or a toddler.

- Even if your child loves technology.

- Even if your child is extremely active and athletic.

- Even if your child is struggling to learn how to read.

- Even if your child *can* read but won't open a book unless it is assigned by a teacher.

In fact, you can change your child's future just by reading this book. Why? Because this book will change your attitude about reading—and your attitude will have an enormous impact on your child's eventual reading success.

My confidence in you isn't based on guesswork or loopy optimism. It comes from a huge body of scientific research as well as my own experiences as a remedial English teacher and a mother.

Reading is no longer a mystery to scientists. They have determined that learning to read is a gradual process that begins at home in infancy and continues through the school years. The problem is, their findings still haven't spread from the research community to the general public, so there is a wide chasm between what scientists have learned and what parents know about reading. Which is why I have written this book—to help bridge the gap between scientists and busy parents like you.

Benefits of The Five Steps

Since I believe science can take us only so far when it comes to parenting, I have combined the best scientific research on the subject with what I learned over the years as a teacher and a mother. From all this, I have extracted five simple steps that make raising a reader very doable.

1 *Talk, Talk, Talk to Your Infant, Toddler, and School-Age Child*

2 *Encourage Free Play and Fiercely Protect Free Time*

3 *Read to Your Child and Expand How, When, and What You Read Aloud*

4 *Support and Motivate Your New Reader and Give Extra Support to Your Struggling Reader*

5 *Use—Don't Abuse—Technology and Balance Your Child's Diet of Fun*

These steps are not meant to be exact prescriptions; rather, they offer you a new way of thinking about reading. You can use them in any order you wish, and adapt them to your specific needs, personality, and circumstances.

Once you have read this book, you will know:

- Which popular ideas about children and reading are myths.

- When the word "early" does—and doesn't—matter in reading.

- What bag of tricks helps all children—pre-readers, precocious readers, as well as those with reading difficulties—become life-long book lovers.

- When to stay relaxed about your child's reading ability and when to aggressively advocate for him.

- How to help your child get the most from technology.

Pleasure Is the Key

Too often, adults approach the subject of reading with a rather grim take-your-medicine-because-it's-good-for-you attitude. My approach is the exact opposite. It is based on a fascinating discovery I made when I was teaching: Although learning to read is serious business, raising a reader is mostly about monkey business—playfulness, laughter, affection, flights of fancy, and joy.

So I want to make something clear from the start. My approach to raising readers is grounded in science. But my method hinges on pleasure—pleasure for parents and pleasure for children, pleasure now and pleasure in the future.

If you take these five simple steps with your infant, toddler, or school-age child, you will not have to teach or tutor, nor push or pressure him about reading. You will simply invite him to a party—a party in his own mind. If the two of you have enough fun together during his childhood, the party will last his entire life.

> **My approach to raising readers is grounded in science. But my method hinges on pleasure."**

Chapter 1 Review

Main Points

- Your child's ability to read will affect just about every aspect of his life—his intelligence, self-confidence, relationships, career path, economic level, social status, level of inner satisfaction, and health.

- Raising an enthusiastic reader is easier than you realize.

- Your own attitude toward reading matters.

Actions

▶ Be confident that you can help your child learn to love words and reading.

▶ Approach reading as fun, not as work.

Chapter 2

Ignore the Myths About Reading!

Several wildly popular—but false—ideas about children and reading have made parents feel so frustrated and demoralized that some have even stopped trying to interest their children in books and reading. So I want to take a few moments to zero in on these misunderstandings and misconceptions to make sure they don't hold you back from raising a passionate reader.

The myths tend to fall into three separate categories:

1 *Myths about technology*

2 *Myths about teachers and school*

3 *Myths about time*

Let's break these ideas down and see why they are wrong.

Technology

Myth: Kids don't read because of competition from technology.

Technology is a convenient scapegoat, but it is not preventing your child from becoming a reader.

First of all, it makes no sense to think of this as an either/or situation: Either your child will use technology or read books. Your child needs both skills—the ability to use machines and read well—to flourish in our society. Fortunately, since machines and books are not mutually exclusive, she can use technology at one point in the day and read a book at another time and enjoy both activities on a regular basis. But the operative word here is "enjoy," and that's what you need to focus on.

The fact that your child enjoys digital entertainment more than she enjoys reading shouldn't surprise or discourage you. After all, TVs and computers are so easy to use that even a toddler can turn them on and have instant fun. Reading, on the other hand, is an enormously complex, challenging, and demanding cognitive undertaking. A child needs years of instruction and years of practice to learn how to read a book—and in the beginning, reading is very hard work.

A new reader has to spend so much mental energy on the mechanics of sounding out words that she can't focus on the story—so reading feels like drudgery. But this is what you need to understand: If she gets enough practice, she will eventually develop the ability to glance at words and comprehend them in a flash, and reading will feel effortless. Once a child becomes an effortless reader, opening a book will be as relaxing and enjoyable as watching TV and playing video games.

In other words, it's a waste of time to vilify technology. Instead, use The Five Steps in this book to help your child get over the hurdle of the beginning stage of reading so she learns to read with great pleasure by the end of grade school. Once reading becomes second nature to her, she will be able to enjoy technology and enjoy reading books for the rest of her life.

Myth: Technology has taken over children's lives, and there's nothing parents can do about it.

You have an enormous amount of power to determine the impact of technology on your child.

To start with, digital equipment doesn't sneak into your child's life all by itself. You buy entertainment machines, set them up in various rooms of your house, install them in your car, and give them to your child as gifts. Therefore, you can control the amount of technology in your child's environment.

Second, you can prevent your child from overdosing on techno-entertainment the way you prevent her from overdosing on other temptations, such as junk food—by making rules about how, when, and where she can use machines.

Third, you can be a role model by using technology judiciously.

The combination of your actions, decisions, and behavior has a tremendous impact on your child.

It comes down to making a choice: You can take steps to ensure that technology will enhance your child's life, or you can passively allow her to overuse technology and be harmed. Your child, your choice.

Myth: Reading books is a thing of the past in our technological society.

Reading is more important than ever. Why? Because reading is the key to becoming educated, and education is the only path to success in our society.

Americans used to be able to make a comfortable living with just a high school education. But the advent of digital technology and global trading, and a depressed world economy have caused low-wage jobs to dwindle. These days, Americans need college—and even graduate diplomas—just to make it into the middle class. Educational attainment does more than boost income; it is also associated with good health and longevity, and a better quality of life.

In fact, life has become so complex in recent years that reading is needed just to function on a basic everyday level. People must be able to read job applications, training material, instruction manuals, medical and pharmaceutical information, insurance forms, rental and sales documents, and myriad other legal papers in the course of normal life.

A child who does not learn to read well enough to become educated faces a grim future.

Teachers and Schools

Myth: Schools should teach children to read at an early age.

Some parents mistakenly believe they can boost children onto the academic fast track by pressuring nursery schools to start teaching children to read at an early age. But reading researchers have determined that how early children learn to read isn't particularly important. In fact, pushing children to learn to read too early can cause, rather than prevent, reading problems.

> ❝ *How early children learn to read isn't particularly important.*❞

The word "early," however, does play an important part in the reading process in two ways:

First, if you introduce your child to letters, words, and books at an early age (between birth and age five), she will have an easier time learning to read in first grade than if she does not have this foundation.

Second, if your child has difficulty learning to read, early intervention by a trained professional is extremely effective. The earlier a problem is identified, the easier it is to correct.

In other words, switch your focus from when your child learns to read to helping her become a skilled reader over time at the right time.

Myth: Reading happens in school when teachers give reading instruction.

Learning to read is a long, slow process that starts years before a child enters first grade.

You—not classroom teachers—are your child's first reading teacher. You automatically take on this role when you say your first words to your infant, and you help her develop important pre-reading skills during infancy and toddlerhood by talking, singing, and reading out loud to her in the course of everyday life.

You continue to play an important role in the reading process once your child starts school, and you become a partner of her teachers. Teachers introduce new reading skills in the classroom, but then it is up to you to help your child master those skills at home.

All told, you can have a tremendous impact on your child's eventual reading ability by supporting her before and after she starts school.

Myth: Parents should leave the whole responsibility of reading to teachers.

You need to stay in the reading loop and keep a close eye on your child's progress in reading whether she attends a neighborhood public school or a luxe private academy, learns to read easily or has a reading glitch, has excellent or inept teachers. Here is why:

Most teachers are hard working and well meaning, and many are very talented professionals. But studies show that an alarming number of teachers have not been trained in up-to-date methods of teaching reading. And remember, early-grade teachers are busy with a variety of responsibilities. Reading is only one of several subjects they must teach. In addition, the recent trend of standardized testing has put pressure on teachers to devote a large chunk of classroom time to test preparation, which means they have less time than ever to teach reading. So even an able, dedicated, well-trained teacher may not always have time to give your child the individual attention she needs, or to realize that she is struggling with reading—especially if your child is adept at hiding her problem. Furthermore, if the teacher does notice the problem, she may not know how to correct it.

Making matters worse, some school districts still use outmoded reading programs, either because local school boards are reluctant to spend money on replacing teaching materials and retraining teachers, or because old habits die hard. While most children can learn the basics of reading no matter what kind of program is used, an ineffective or inappropriate program can spell disaster for a child with a reading problem.

Since you know your child better than anyone else and are focused solely on her, you may be able to pick up on a reading issue that is being overlooked or mishandled in school. By staying in touch with your child's teachers and making it clear that you consider yourself a partner in the reading process, you can help them do a better job and protect your child from years of unnecessary suffering because of reading difficulties.

Myth: Teachers will instill a love of reading in your child.

Teachers are focused on teaching your child how to read in the classroom. But it is up to you to help your child hold on to her enthusiasm for reading while she is learning to read.

Just about all little children love books and can't wait to learn how to read. But learning to read is such a long and difficult undertaking that children commonly forget that books are fun and stop associating them with pleasure.

If you share the fun of words and books with your child while she is on the road to developing reading skills, she will remain enthusiastic about reading and will be motivated to practice and step up to the next level.

Time

Myth: Parents need extra time to help children become readers.

Raising a reader isn't about spending extra time on reading; it's about being aware of the importance of language in your child's life and being willing to have fun in ways that enhance her language development. Most of the activities I suggest in this book require no extra time—and even the few that do require your undivided attention can be done in short sessions.

The truth is, raising a reader will save you time. If your child is an enthusiastic reader, she will do her schoolwork without difficulty, and you will not have to nag her about homework, help her complete assignments, or deal with teachers about her academic issues (plus, you'll be spared the heartache of having a child who hates school and feels terrible about herself).

> " *The truth is, raising a reader will save you time.*"

Reading difficulties can cause an avalanche of emotional and academic complications that are costly in a multitude of ways. It will be infinitely less time consuming to help your young child get on the right track in reading in the first place than it will be to help her get back on track if she falls off the academic rails in the upper grades.

Chapter 2 Review

Main Points

- Using technology and reading can go together. Your child needs both skills. Vilifying technology is a waste of time.

- You have an enormous amount of power to determine the impact of technology on your child. Control the amount of technology in your child's environment, prevent your child from overdosing on technology, and be a role model by using technology judiciously yourself.

- Reading is more important than ever in our society. It is the key to becoming educated, and education is the only path to success.

- When a child learns to read isn't particularly important. Pushing children to read too early can actually cause reading problems rather than prevent them.

- You are your child's first reading teacher. It is up to you to introduce your child to words and help her develop pre-reading skills. Once she starts school, you become a partner with her teachers.

- While it is the job of your child's teacher to teach reading in the classroom, it is up to you to help your child hold on to her enthusiasm for reading and remind her that reading is fun.

● It will take less time to help your young child get on the right track to literacy in the first place than to help her get back on track if she falls off the academic rails in the upper grades.

Actions

▶ Set limits so your child doesn't overdose on technology.

▶ Be a role model for your child by using technology judiciously.

▶ Introduce your child to letters, words, and books at an early age.

▶ If your child has difficulty learning to read, early intervention is extremely effective.

▶ Keep a close eye on your child's progress in reading and consider yourself a partner with her teacher.

▶ Encourage your child to use words and books for fun.

Part 2

The Five Steps

Chapter 3

Step One:
Talk, Talk, Talk to Your Infant, Toddler, and School-Age Child

The easiest, most effective way to help your child become a reader is to talk to him and share words in other ways in your everyday life: sing, read aloud, rhyme, rap, ask riddles, tell jokes, make up stories and poems, chat while cooking, and play games. Words are like vitamins for your child's developing brain.

The more words a child hears, sees, and uses, the smarter he gets and the easier it is for him to become a reader.

Words are like vitamins for your child's developing brain."

Brainpower: Use It or Lose It

Scientists used to believe the brain was a fixed, unchanging organ. They assumed the brain a child was born with remained the same throughout his whole life. But in recent decades, researchers have learned that the human brain is far more plastic and subject to environmental influences than was previously understood. They now know that a child's inherited genes can be switched on or off depending on his surroundings. In other words, experience changes the brain.

Your child was born with trillions of neural connections and billions of brain cells. But his brain will develop according to a use-it-or-lose-it principle. If you expose him to a great deal of language stimulation in his everyday life (because you talk, sing, read aloud, etc.), you will activate his language centers, and this brain wiring will become a permanent part of his neurological connections. If he does not get this kind of stimulation, his brain will gradually prune unused wiring and leave him with fewer neural connections and a diminished ability to learn how to talk, read, and write. As neuroscientists like to say: Cells that fire together, wire together.

" The more words a child hears, sees, and uses, the smarter he gets and the easier it is for him to become a reader."

The Hart-Risley Study

The impact of everyday conversations and interactions on young children was first documented in the 1980s by two Kansas professors, Betty Hart and Todd Risley. The researchers spent years recording and analyzing the number and types of words parents used when talking to infants and toddlers in three different kinds of families—professional, working class, and welfare. After analyzing all the data, they concluded that by age four, children in professional homes had heard forty-six million words, in blue-collar homes they had heard twenty-six million words, and in welfare homes they had heard thirteen million words.

Hart and Risley also discovered that when professional parents spoke to their children, they used complex sentences, a rich vocabulary, and a lot of positive feedback (Great! Nice job! Good boy!), whereas parents on welfare frequently used words of disapproval (Stop! No! Don't!). When all the children were tested at age four and again at age nine, there was a strong positive correlation between the number and quality of words children heard at home and their IQ levels, reading ability, and success in school.

Why Sharing Words Helps Your Child Learn to Read

The first reading skill your child will be taught in school is how to sound out words—a challenging mental process that involves several steps. First, he must break each word into its smallest units of sound (for example, the word *"sat"* has three distinct sounds—suh/aa/tuh). Next, he must recombine the parts and silently say the word in his mind. Then he has to search his memory for the meaning of the word. Finally, he must store the word in his memory for future use.

Studies show that the more knowledge a child has about alphabetic letters, words, and books before he enters first grade, the easier it is for him to learn how to sound out words. Therefore, the more you expose your infant or toddler to language by singing, chatting, reading aloud, rhyming, and making up stories, the more he will learn about language and the easier it will be for him to learn the first steps in reading.

" *The more knowledge a child has about alphabetic letters, words, and books before he enters first grade, the easier it is for him to learn how to sound out words."*

But sounding out words isn't reading. Reading is the process of sounding out and comprehending words. For example, if your child can sound out the word "igloo" but doesn't know what an igloo is, he can't read that word. But if he has heard the word during casual conversations with you or when you read a book aloud, he knows what the word means. The more you talk to your child and the more books you read aloud to him, the bigger his vocabulary grows and the easier it is for him to make sense of many words.

And there is one additional way that sharing words with

your child makes it easier for him to become a reader: It helps him develop the skill of making inferences—the ability to "read between the lines." This is a subtle skill that takes years to develop, but unless a reader learns how to make inferences, he won't understand the author's intention and the characters' motivations.

For example, if your child encounters the sentence, "Charlie's face turned bright red," he needs to discern whether Charlie is angry, embarrassed, ill, or sunburned. How does he do this? By using his knowledge of the world to interpret clues in the text. If red-faced Charlie is shouting and waving a fist in the air, your child understands that Charlie is angry; if Charlie just looked down at his feet and noticed he's wearing two different colored shoes, your child gets that Charlie is blushing from embarrassment. The more your child knows about the world and about human behavior, the easier it will be for him to interpret descriptions. Where does he learn this information? Through informal, everyday conversations with you and other adults and from hearing books read aloud.

Sharing words in a variety of ways before and after your child learns to read will:

- Activate brain wiring in his language centers and increase the capacity of his brain.

- Make it easier for him to learn how to sound out words in first grade.

- Increase his vocabulary, which will enable him to make sense of words.

- Help him develop the skill of making inferences so he can interpret the meaning of material he is reading.

My Lucky Accident

I stumbled across the amazing outcome of talking to infants by accident when I was a new, very inexperienced mother. I loved my adorable baby, but I confess that I found it somewhat mind-numbing to spend long stretches of time with him. So I entertained myself by having long interchanges with him, during which I'd do both sides of our conversation (*"What did you think about the President's speech last night? You loved it? Me, too. Think he'll win the election?"*). I also narrated our activities (*"Okay, we're coming into the final stretch of the international diaper changing contest."*), pointed out unusual sights (*"Yikes, look at the guy with the monkey on his shoulder."*), sang nonsense songs, (*"Hickory, dickory, dock, the sheep ate the cackling clock."*), rhymed (*"I take off the dipe, then wipe and swipe."*), read aloud while feeding him, and put on silly puppet shows with washcloths, oven mitts, socks, shoes, stuffed animals, and salt and pepper shakers. I was mostly trying to keep my brain alive—but I suspected that my shenanigans might benefit my son in some way.

Then something shocking happened when he was eight months old: I tucked him into his carriage on a crisp fall morning, told him it was perfect weather for deep breathing, sucked in my breath, then let it out with a theatrical *whoosh*. The baby, a contemplative little guy, furrowed his brow and stared at me so intently that I repeated my performance before I set out for the park near our apartment. When we returned home several hours later, I murmured in passing, *"Okay, we'll do more deep breathing tomorrow,"* and the baby opened his tiny mouth and panted. I gawked at him in amazement. *Oh my god,* I remember thinking, *there's a human in there ... and he knows what I'm talking about!* Then suddenly I realized that my verbal playfulness had helped him connect the sounds he heard me utter and an idea. After that, I took our fun together very seriously, and used words as toys through his infancy, toddlerhood, and grade school years. And I did the same thing with my other two sons after they were born. At the time, I didn't know how my playfulness helped them, I just knew my animated methods were clearly effective.

Two decades later, when I came across a scientific article trumpeting the news that exposure to language increases a child's brain wiring, I finally understood why my playfulness with language had helped my three children become excellent readers.

You Have a Window of Opportunity

There is a critical period for language development that begins in infancy and ends sometime between age eight and puberty. The more language stimulation a child receives during this critical period, the more functional wiring his brain develops and the more language ability he acquires.

You can raise your child's IQ and make it easier for him to learn to read if you:

- Expose him to a great number and variety of words from his birth through his teens.
- Encourage him to talk.
- Give him choices often as you can about everything from ice cream to T-shirts, and ask him to explain his choices.
- Ask questions that make him think.
- Answer questions patiently rather than snappishly.
- Explain your answers to his questions.

Creating a language-rich environment for your child is not difficult or time consuming. In fact, if you're a naturally talkative person, you're probably doing many of these things already. If, however, you are used to keeping your thoughts and feelings to yourself, you may have to tweak your personality a bit to become more vocal and outgoing. But whatever your personality, it's easy to increase the number and variety of words you share with your child—and the payoff is huge. Goodness knows, you can afford to be generous with words since there are more than five hundred thousand words in the English language!

In this chapter I offer eight different ways you can interact with your child to help him get off to a great start with words. You don't have to do them all. Choose the ones that are right for you and your child—the ones you are actually likely to do. But please do them, because they work!

Easy Ways to Increase Your Child's Exposure to Words

1. Hang up interesting pictures and chat about them.

Your infant or child will spend thousands of hours at home during the next few years. While it's lovely to pay attention to the interior decoration of your house or apartment, it's more important to pay attention to the interior decoration of your child's brain, heart, and soul by talking with him.

You can add snap and sizzle to everyday conversations by hanging interesting pictures, postcards, maps, or photographs on walls and on the refrigerator and chatting about them. Even brief comments or questions will stimulate your child's brain, expand his vocabulary, broaden his knowledge of the world, and encourage his curiosity—all of which will help him become a reader (the pictures will also give him something to think about when you're not in the room).

You can buy posters and pictures, download images from the Internet, or cut out photographs and drawings from magazines, newspapers, catalogs, or pamphlets. The less time and money you spend on hanging things up, the better off you will be. If you invest too much in something, you won't want to take it down, and your reactions to the images will grow stale. New pictures generate new ideas and keep conversations fresh and lively.

When my kids were growing up, I plastered the walls and the refrigerator door with colorful or arresting pictures I cut out of magazines; posters I bought in book stores, museum gift shops, and teacher supply houses; postcards my friends sent from exotic countries; travel brochures; color charts from paint stores; and fabric remnants.

"Add snap and sizzle to everyday conversations by hanging interesting pictures."

I once hung a picture of a multicolored parrot over my infant son's changing table so he wouldn't wiggle around while I diapered him. I had animated conversations with Mr. Parrot. (*"You think my hair looks like a rat's nest? That's a rude, insulting thing to say!"*) Of course my son didn't understand most of what I said, but he heard lots of words and got the gist of what I was saying from my tone and facial expressions, and in any case, he thoroughly enjoyed my antics—and stayed still while I diapered him.

At another point, I tacked up a sneaker ad (after cutting off the brand name) because it had photographs of legs that belonged to different people or creatures: a ballerina, a racehorse, a basketball player, an ice skater, a centipede, and a jogger. This gave me a chance to chat with my toddler about feet, dancing, ballet, hooves, racetracks, sneakers, ice skating, and insects, which widened his vocabulary and added to his general knowledge of the world.

When my sons got older, they took control of their bedroom walls. But even their choices of pictures and posters would be fodder for conversation. For example, when they hung a circus poster that had a picture of the glamorous lion tamer we'd recently seen perform (who looked like a blonde Elvis replete with long platinum ponytail, white diamond-studded jumpsuit, silver shoes, and silver whip), we chatted about why people choose dangerous professions, risk-taking, human-animal relationships, fear, courage, power, control, and the challenge of keeping a white jumpsuit clean in a cage full of lions.

Confession: I wrecked the walls of our apartment by continuously tacking and taping up new pictures. But I figured it would be easier to spackle and repaint the walls than to redecorate my sons' brains after they grew up. And if you're not as slapdash as I am, you can use cork bulletin boards to protect your walls.

Here are three examples of conversations prompted by pictures on a child's wall:

With an infant: *"Look at this picture of snowflakes drifting down from the sky onto the pine trees. See the gray squirrel in the tree?"*

With a toddler: *"That mouse on the poster has such a mischievous expression. Do you think he's planning to steal that hunk of cheese on the table?"*

With a grade-school child: *"Isn't that a breathtaking photograph of hikers on Mount Everest? Do you think professional climbers get so used to heights that they're like, 'Ho-hum, another day hanging from the edge of a precipice'?"* (When your child asks the inevitable, *"What's a pressapish?"* You can say, *"Cliff!"*)

2. Narrate your life in real time: Explain what you're doing and why you're doing it.

Talk about your movements and actions when you're doing everyday chores like cleaning the kitchen, changing a light bulb, or unloading groceries after a shopping expedition. Even when you talk about simple things, you help your child's language centers to grow new wiring.

You can give a straight narration of the facts (*"I'm going to take out the garbage before the rain starts"*) or let your imagination soar and pretend you're someone else—a TV newscaster, magician, queen, or frog (*"I'm tying up this bag of gold and taking it out to the cave before the dragon gets here and tries to steal it!"*).

Here are some examples:

While diapering an infant: *"I'm changing your wet diaper so you won't get a rash. Now I'm putting on your blue striped overalls and matching shirt that grandma sent you. This baby powder smells so sweet on your tummy. Wow, you look adorable. I think blue is a super color for you."*

While food shopping with a toddler: *"I'm putting one, two, three yogurts into the wagon. And I'll add a carton of milk and a dozen eggs. Now we'll go over to the produce department for fruits and vegetables. Do you know the name of the yellow fruit hanging from that hook? That's right—bananas."*

While driving with a grade-school child: *"We'd better stop at the garage on our way home because I hit a pothole this morning, and we need to check the tires. I wonder why the high-way's jammed this early in the day. Maybe there's an accident up ahead. I wish we could turn the car into a plane and zoom above the traffic. Okay, captain, get ready to retract the wheels, hit the button to spread the car's hidden wings, and prepare for takeoff!"*

3. Use colorful words and descriptive details to paint word pictures.

Avoid vague, clichéd descriptions and give your child specific, quirky, or playful depictions of events or places. Have fun with words.

Here are some examples:

Tell an infant: *"The smoke from the chimney is coiling into the air like a snake."*

Tell a toddler: *"Look at that rabbit munching on the grass. His front teeth are so big; maybe he should visit an orthodontist. But I guess if his teeth were fixed, he'd look more like a weird long-eared cat than a rabbit."*

Tell a grade-school child: *"The movie I saw last night had a hilarious food fight scene in an Italian restaurant. Pizzas zoomed through the air like flying saucers, tomato sauce was splattered on the walls, gooey cheese dripped from the ceiling, and pizzas flew out the window."*

4. Encourage questions and explain your answers.

When your child asks a question, restate his question and explain your answer.

Tell an infant: *"No, honey, you can't hold the screwdriver because it has a sharp point, and it might hurt you."*

Tell a toddler: *"Yes, you can have one more ride on the merry-go-round. But after that, we have to go home so you can have your nap."*

Tell a grade-school child: *"No, you can't have another candy bar because we're eating dinner soon, and I don't want you to ruin your appetite."*

5. Ask questions that encourage your child to think and talk about abstract ideas.

Phrase questions so they can't be answered with a simple yes or no, and encourage your child to use a wide range of words.

Instead of asking an infant: *"See the puppy?"*

Ask: *"Why do you think the puppy is wagging his tail? That's right, he's feeling happy."*

Instead of asking a toddler: *"Did you have fun at the playground?"*

Ask: *"What did you do at the playground?"*

Instead of asking a grade-school child: *"Do you like your new teacher?"*

Ask: *"What is your new teacher like?"*

6. Use letters and words as toys.

Play a short, simple word game with your child while you're riding together in the car, on a bus or train, sharing a snack, or walking the dog.

Here are some letter/word games you might play.

With an infant or toddler:

Sing or chant the alphabet ("a-b-c-d...")

Play with magnetic letters. Leave colorful magnetic letters on the refrigerator door. Point out individual letters and say their sounds. Help your child rearrange the letters to make words.

Say the sound of the letter. Say a word, tell your baby the sound of the first letter, and repeat the word. (*"This is your toe. Toe starts with a tuh sound. Toe."*)

What's the sound? Ask your toddler to tell you the first sound of a word. (*"What's the first sound of boot? That's right, buh."*)

Find the letter. Say the sound of a letter and ask your toddler to find the letter in a book or on road or store signs. (*"E. That's right, exit starts with an e."*)

Same letter. Pick a letter, say its sound, and ask your child to name two objects in the room that begin or end with it. (*"What objects in the room start with r? That's right, radiator and rug start with r. What object ends with a d? Good, food and lid end with a d."*)

Opposites. Say a word and ask your child for its opposite. (*Tall/ short, hot/cold, happy/sad.*)

Similars. Say a word and ask your child for a similar word. (*Happy/glad, frightening/scary, loud/noisy.*)

With a grade-school child:

Tell a story. Make up a sentence, ask your child to add the next sentence, and continue to take turns. (*"That parking meter is really a Martian./ He likes to eat quarters and dimes./ At night he climbs into his space ship and flies around."*)

Make up new words for old songs. (*"Go go go your goat gently down the beam."*)

Memorize together. Commit poems, lists, and favorite literary passages to memory. (*"The names of the Seven Dwarfs are Sneezy, Happy, Sleepy, uh, Irving?"*)

Estimate the amount/distance/time. Ask your child to make a wild guess about something and compare it to your guess. (*"How many steps will it take us to get to the end of the street?"* or *"How many jelly beans do you think are in that jar?"*)

7. Rhyme, rhyme, rhyme.

Little children love hearing and chanting rhymes, which is why Jack and Jill who went up the hill, Little Bo Peep who lost her sheep, and Jack Sprat who could eat no fat have been popular for generations.

But rhyming does more than entertain infants and toddlers; it helps them develop important skills they will need in order to become readers. Here is why rhyming is so important:

The first reading skill a child is taught in grade school is sounding out words, a complicated mental process that consists of several steps. A child must recognize the look and sound of individual letters of the alphabet, break the word into its smallest units of sound, recombine the separate units, and silently say the word to himself. Rhyming familiarizes a child with the sounds of letters and allows him to practice breaking words into small segments.

The more rhyming your child does before he goes to school, the easier it will be for him to learn how to sound out words in first grade. Here are easy ways to weave rhyming games into your everyday life:

Read nursery rhymes aloud. Read nursery rhymes and rhyming poems during your child's infancy and continue reading rhymes and poems aloud through grade school. (*"Hickory dickory dock/ the mouse ran up the clock."*)

Make up your own rhymes about daily life. (*"We're walking to the train./I hope it doesn't rain." "We're driving in the car,/but we won't go very far."*)

Sing songs that rhyme. Sing famous songs or create your own rhyming lyrics. (*"You're my little bunny./You're just as sweet as honey."*)

Play short, rhyming word games. Say a word and ask your child for a word that rhymes with it. (*"Big/dig; art/heart; I/spy."*)

Play rhyming story games. Make up a line of a story and ask your child to add a rhyming sentence. (*"The castle door was big and green./It looked just like a big string bean."*)

> *The more rhyming your child does before he goes to school, the easier it will be for him to learn how to sound out words in first grade."*

8. Play short, simple writing games.

When you have a moment at home or are sitting in a doctor's office or waiting for a pizza, take a scrap of paper—a napkin, the back of an envelope, or a paper grocery bag will do—and invite your child to play a short writing game with you. If he's too young to write, let him dictate his answers and you do all the writing. If he knows how to write, he can jot down his answers himself. If he knows how to write but doesn't feel like writing, act as his scribe and do the writing for him. (And don't accuse him of being lazy. This isn't school. The whole point is to make it as easy as possible for him to have fun with words.) When he loses interest, stop playing. If it's not fun, it's not a game. Here are some games you can play:

Body writing. Trace a letter or letters on your child's back with your finger and ask him to tell you what you've written. Reverse roles. (*"Uh, I think you just wrote h-e-l-l-o—hello."*)

"I challenge you" game. Write down an easy word and challenge your child to read it. If he succeeds, change one letter to create a similar word. Build his confidence by using simple words. (*"That says 'big.' That says 'bid.' That says 'hid.' That says 'did.'"*)

Rearrange words. Write a word, then ask your child to rearrange the letters to make new words out of it. (*"Bunch: nub/hun; Live: evil/lie/vile."*)

Description game. Ask your child to look at something or someone and write down three words to describe him/her/it. You do the same thing. Then compare your lists. (*"That dog looks: cute, skinny, lost/obedient, starving, old." "Our waitress* *seems: grouchy, witchy, angry/grumpy, hostile, tired.*")

Write lists of things adored/things abhorred. (*"I hate itchy sweaters, slimy worms, salty food/I love cats, candy, Christmas."*)

Write a book. Nothing fancy, nothing complicated. Take a sheet of paper and fold it in half or staple a few pieces of paper together. Then ask your child to help you write a short book and draw a picture on its cover. You can take turns doing the writing and drawing the illustrations, but give your child full control of the project. It doesn't matter whether his story is funny or serious—or even makes sense. What matters is the fun involved in creating a book. When it is finished, read it out loud to him and to others in the family, then hang it on the wall for everyone to admire.

Write a handbook of myths. (*"When a tooth falls out, put it under your pillow and the Tooth Fairy will exchange it for money." "Four-leaf clovers are lucky." "Black cats are unlucky."*)

Make a book of your own silly myths. (*"If you bury an olive in moonlight, it will turn into a dog."*)

Draw and label new inventions. Ask your child to design, draw, and name a new machine or make improvements to the human body. (*"I'm drawing a body that has two heads, feet that swivel, eyes on both hands, and ears on the knees. What are you drawing?"*)

Create short scavenger hunts. Hide a treasure, treat, or funny note in your house and write simple clues that will help your child find it. (*"Enter a room that has a broom."/"Look in the shoe that is blue."*)

Create a newspaper. Ask your child to interview family members and write up the latest gossip. (*"Grandpa turns eighty next Sunday! Birthday party in our backyard."*)

Run an election for president of your child's room. Ask your child to help you write/deliver short campaign speeches on behalf of dolls and stuffed animals who want to be "candidates." (*"As the biggest dog in this room, I promise everyone in America a bone!"/"I may have long ears and a cotton tail, but I'm no dumb bunny!"*)

Help your child write a letter to the Tooth Fairy. (*"Dear Ms. Toothie, I'm leaving my tooth under my pillow for you. Please note that the value of the U.S. dollar has fallen, and the cost of living has risen. So please consider increasing your rate of exchange."*)

Create and label a dream house. Ask your child to help you draw the perfect house for kids and label each room and gadget. (*"Candy Room—open 24/7," "Mommy Robot—press button and she will always say 'Yes'."*)

"Spice up" a book. Ask your child to "improve" a book by crossing out some words and substituting new words. (But only write in books you own! Never, never, never deface a school or library book.)

Chapter 3 Review

Main Points

- The more words a child hears, sees, and uses, the smarter he gets and the easier it is for him to become a skilled reader.

- If you expose your child to a lot of language, you will activate his language centers, and this brain wiring will become a permanent part of his neurological connections.

- There is a high correlation between the number and quality of words children hear at home and their IQ levels, reading ability, and success in school.

- The more knowledge a child has about the letters of the alphabet, words, and books before he enters first grade, the easier it will be for him to learn how to sound out words.

- Sharing words in a variety of ways before and after your child learns to read will help him to sound out words, build vocabulary, and develop the ability to make inferences so he can interpret the meaning of what he reads.

- There is a critical period for language development that begins in infancy and ends sometime between the age of eight and puberty. The more language stimulation a child receives during this critical period, the more functional wiring his brain develops, and the more language ability he acquires.

Actions

► Talk to your child and share words in other ways in your normal everyday life: sing, read aloud, rhyme, rap, ask riddles, tell jokes, make up stories and poems, chat while cooking, and play games. Give your child choices as often as you can, and ask him to explain his choices.

► Hang up interesting pictures and chat with your child about them.

► Narrate your life in real time. Explain what you're doing and why you're doing it.

► Use colorful words to paint word pictures.

► Encourage questions and explain your answers. Answer your child's questions patiently.

► Ask questions that encourage your child to think and talk about abstract ideas.

► Use letters and words as toys.

► Rhyme with your child.

► Play short, simple writing games.

Chapter 4

Step Two: Encourage Free Play and Fiercely Protect Free Time

You may think it's ridiculous for me to bring up the subject of play in a book about reading. But you can make it easier for your child to become a reader, develop her social and emotional skills, and succeed in life just by encouraging her to engage in free play—and by that I mean "old-fashioned" play that involves people and objects in the real world.

Let me backtrack for a minute and say that play is valuable simply because it's fun; it doesn't need more justification than that. But new studies by cognitive psychologists tell us that play is a vital part of a child's intellectual, physical, and social development. In fact, playing and learning are so entwined that it's difficult to separate the two. A child instinctively plays to learn and learns by playing; the more she plays, the more stimulation she gives her brain, and the smarter she gets. Play is nature's way of helping a child build enough intelligence to survive life's challenges.

Researchers have also learned that free play increases a child's executive function—the part of her brain that enables her to process and store information, organize thoughts, control impulses, avoid distraction, and focus on a single task to completion. Some studies have found a strong correlation between a child's ability to control her emotional and cognitive impulses and academic success—as well as success in adult life.

Why Free Play Is Beneficial

Every kind of play—including digital activities—can help your child build new skills. But free play is especially beneficial because it involves all five senses and stimulates neural wiring that runs from head to toe, thereby turning her whole body— not just her brain—into a vehicle for learning.

When your infant babbles and coos, kicks her feet, waves her hands, crawls and rolls over, she is learning about her body. When your toddler examines objects in the house, explores the backyard, performs experiments with toys and cups of water in the bath, and digs in the sand, she is learning about her environment. When your school-age child plays games alone or with others, she learns about risk taking, winning, losing, following rules, and getting along with both adults and children.

Unstructured, three-dimensional play

- Stimulates new brain wiring.

- Increases a child's ability to concentrate.

- Expands her capacity to learn new skills.

- Widens knowledge of the world.

- Enhances problem-solving skills.

- Fosters patience, creativity, curiosity, perseverance, empathy, and self-control.

- Reinforces a natural appetite for learning.

All of these things will make it easier for your child to become a lifelong reader and learner.

Free play is especially beneficial because it involves all five senses and stimulates neural wiring that runs from head to toe, thereby turning her whole body—not just her brain—into a vehicle for learning."

Study Your Child at Play

If you haven't thought about how much your child is learning while she is playing, take a few moments to study her when she's doing an activity as simple as building a sand castle. It doesn't matter whether she's a toddler in a sandbox or a preteen on a beach: the process of learning through play is the same at any age.

On one level, she's simply having fun. But watch her closely and you'll realize that she is exercising her creativity, imagination, and intelligence to plan a project, breaking a large task into smaller segments, and prioritizing her work. If she makes a mistake and her castle collapses, she has to deal with disappointment and rethink what she is doing in order to correct her error. If she succeeds in attaining her goal, she learns the value of patience and persistence. If she is unable to finish the castle, she has to deal with frustration and failure. If another child joins her, she gets a chance to practice her communication skills, learns to follow rules, develops the ability to negotiate conflicts, and increases her capacity for empathy. In other words, while she is "just" having fun, she is also developing a range of skills and character traits that will enhance the quality of her life.

Warning: Free Play Is Becoming Extinct

Unfortunately, the amount of time American children have for free play has been shrinking in recent years. Adults are busier than ever. The number of children living in one-parent homes has increased. Standardized testing emphasizes academic achievement over fun. Parents no longer feel that it's safe for children to play outdoors without close supervision. And technology has come onto the scene in a very big way.

As a result, infants are spending an increasing amount of time in car seats or strollers, sitting and watching TV, and sitting on their parents' laps in front of computers. Toddlers are shuttled from one organized skills class to the next. Public schools are cutting back on recess and gym periods in order to add academic courses. Children are kept busy all day in school—and continue to be busy after school. They attend extended day programs; play on organized sports teams; take music, dance and language lessons; receive religious instruction; get tutored in academic subjects; and are prepped for standardized tests. By the time most children get home, eat dinner, and do their homework, they have very little time left over for free play.

And not only do children have less time for free play, technology has radically altered the way they play. These days, children do not come home from school and rush outdoors to climb trees, build forts, play tag or stickball, roller skate, ride bikes, or jump rope as children did in previous generations. Nor do they play indoors the way children used to play—by building models of ships and planes; collecting stamps, baseball cards, charms, and coins; doing jigsaw puzzles; creating scenes with dolls; painting, drawing, and coloring.

What are they doing? Spending an average of seven and a half hours a day watching TV, playing computer and video games, talking/texting/gaming on smart phones, and using other digital devices.

According to a wide range of educators, psychologists, reading specialists, and medical doctors, this situation is having a dire impact on children's health and well-being. Their research shows that children who do not spend a sufficient amount of time engaging in nontechnological, three-dimensional play are vulnerable to obesity, ADHD, childhood depression, learning disabilities, behavioral issues, and problems in school.

Right now, your young child loves books and has an almost insatiable appetite for learning. She plays and learns, learns and plays from the moment she opens her eyes in the morning until she goes to sleep at night. She uses her mind as a built-in supercomputer that provides her with endless opportunities for fun—and she enjoys books because they help her tap into her fertile imagination.

But as she gets older and her days become increasingly structured, she will have less and less time for uninhibited play. Once she enters grade school and spends her days in the classroom, she may gradually come to associate books and reading with schoolwork and homework, and forget that books are a source of pleasure. If this happens, she will lose her habit of plugging into books for fun and will turn to technology for all relaxation and recreation.

You can prevent this syndrome by encouraging her to engage in lots of free play.

The Challenge of Nurturing Your Young Child's Playfulness

It's easy to talk about the value of play and quite another thing to live day to day with a young child. Taking care of an energetic, curious child can be a joy and delight, but it can also be stressful and exhausting. Why? Because the very trait that helps her survive and grow—her powerful drive to learn—can also lead her into all sorts of mischief.

The situation boils down to this: You have time pressures because of your work, family, social commitments, and responsibilities. But your young child is primarily focused on having fun. Inevitably, when your adult needs intersect with your child's passion for learning and playing—*kaboom!* The emotional fireworks start. For example, when she uses peanut butter as finger paint, spills milk over the edge of her high chair to create a waterfall, or chases a butterfly across a busy parking lot, she isn't thinking about her safety or your convenience and schedule no matter how many warnings you've given her. Her passion for learning overtakes all other thoughts and she's off and running—with you cleaning up or running after her.

This is an important dynamic to understand because your attitude about your child's playfulness, and the way you express your anger and frustration when she disrupts your home or schedule, will have a tremendous impact on her attitude toward learning. While you want to keep her safe and teach her how to follow rules and behave well, you also want to nurture her intellectual curiosity and enjoyment of learning.

After you stop your child from doing something destructive, obnoxious, or inconsiderate, and tell her why her behavior is unacceptable, look for a way to encourage her learning impulse. You might praise her for being curious, creative, or ingenious, or invite her to continue her "experiment" in a more acceptable form. You won't always have the time, energy, or patience to do this, but often it will only take a tiny bit of effort to encourage this valuable trait—and the return will be huge. Here are some examples of what I'm talking about:

Example I:

You discover your child decorating your living room sofa with leftover spaghetti from dinner.

Positive Response: *"You are not allowed to play with food in the living room because it will ruin my furniture. But after you clean up the spaghetti, you can continue your art project in the kitchen sink."*

Negative Response: *"You're going to be punished for making such a horrible mess. Go to your room right now."*

Example 2:

You and your child are late to a doctor's appointment, but she wants to linger in front of a pet shop window.

Positive Response: *"Honey, I know you're fascinated by the puppies, but we have to get to our appointment right now. Let's come back another day when we have enough time to watch the puppies."*

Negative Response: *"Stop daydreaming slowpoke, and get moving!"*

Example 3:

Your child scribbles on the wall with a crayon.

Positive Response: *"You can only use crayons on paper, not on walls. Here's a pad. Draw a picture for me, and we'll hang it up."*

Negative response: *"You've wrecked the walls. No more crayons for you!"*

If you value her learning impulse, she will value it, too.

How to Encourage Free Play

1. Childproof your home.

Your child needs a safe, comfortable environment in which to roam, explore, test, observe, and learn. This doesn't mean you have to turn your whole house into a playroom, but you do need to create some areas where she can play freely without damaging herself, your possessions, or your sanity. If you constantly tell your child, *"Don't touch!"* or, *"Stop that!"* when she's doing what comes naturally, you will squelch her appetite for learning and create tension in your household. You can avoid this negative dynamic by doing the following:

- Remove or anchor wobbly objects such as floor lamps, bookcases, and statues.

- Tie up cords from appliances and window shades so they are out of reach.

- Temporarily cover delicate furniture fabrics.

- Keep valuable or fragile objects out of reach or put them away entirely until your child is older. If you leave a glass vase on the coffee table, your toddler will be tempted to grab it no matter how many times you say, *"Don't touch!"* When your child reaches for something you don't want her to have, don't just say, *"No!"* Instead, tell her, *"No, not a toy."* This will stop her from what she's doing at that moment and teach her that the world is divided into two categories: things she can play with (toys) and things she can't play with (not toys). It will take your infant or toddler time to catch on to this concept, but it will eventually sink in and make life more pleasant for everyone in the household.

2. Equip your house for nontech fun.

Keep a variety of supplies on hand that will give your child the opportunity to create, invent, and experiment. If she's mature enough to follow rules and instructions, store the supplies in an accessible box, drawer, or closet. If she still needs supervision, keep the box out of reach so she doesn't hurt herself or wreck your house. Stock up on:

- Pens, pencils, crayons, markers, watercolors, and brushes.

- Stickers, finger paint, and clay.

- Pads of paper, large sheets of poster paper, and paper bags from stores.

- Round-edged scissors, glue, rubber bands, and tape.

- Dolls, stuffed animals, and action figures.

- Board games, cards, and dominoes.

- Building blocks and balls.

3. Use everyday objects as toys.

Encourage your child to use her imagination to turn common household objects into works of art, games, inventions, and experiments.

- Use old magazines as coloring books or cut them up to make collages.

- Use foam packing material as building blocks.

- Use empty cartons for pretend play (turn them into a sailboat, rocket ship, fort, or castle).

- Use empty cereal or pasta boxes as dollhouses or garages for toy cars and trucks.

- Use old clothing for dress-up games.

4. Do not overschedule your child.

Studies show that infants and young children are excellent at choosing activities that help them learn most efficiently. Resist the pressure to enroll your young child in skills classes that keep her busy all day, and make sure she has time to play freely every day, either alone or with others. She needs a chance to explore natural objects, invent games, use her imagination, and process new information.

Scientists have recently discovered a specific set of brain regions they call the default network, which only becomes active when the rest of the brain is inactive—for example, when we daydream or sleep. So even when your child seems to be doing nothing, her brain is actually working on solving difficult problems, integrating information, and making sense of the world.

5. Express admiration for your child's playfulness.

Let your child know that you value her playfulness and think that having fun is an important part of life, not a waste of time. Compliment her creativity when she makes mud pies, dresses up as a superhero, or builds a snowman. Praise her inventiveness when she turns a scrap of paper into a mini-kite, draws or paints a picture, or experiments with water in the sink or bathtub. Let her know you admire her ability to have fun by using her imagination.

6. Encourage your child's ability to become engaged in activities.

Happiness is a very elusive emotion, and we adults expend a lot of time, effort, and money seeking happiness. But children instinctively understand that happiness comes from deep engagement in an activity and working hard to achieve a goal. As a result, young children are joyful for much of their day.

Your child continuously sets goals for herself when she is playing. Her goals may not seem important or even be apparent to you, but they have meaning for her, and once she achieves them, she sets new goals for herself—just for the sheer pleasure of mastering something new. The enjoyment that comes from being absorbed in a task is the same for a toddler learning how to climb a step, a ten-year-old flying a kite, or a

Nobel Prize-winning scientist testing a new theory in a lab. The learner gets into a "flow" state and loses awareness of her surroundings—an inherently satisfying experience. It is this quality that you want to nurture in your child. It will help her continue to derive great joy from learning throughout her whole life.

7. Encourage regular physical exercise.

Scientists have learned that physical exercise has a far greater impact on children's development than was previously understood. According to recent studies, children who get regular exercise have a greater ability to concentrate and learn new material, do better in school, and have fewer behavioral problems than children who do not exercise on a regular basis.

The brain is an organ of the body and needs exercise to stay in shape. Sedentary behavior will not only limit your child's intellectual and social development, it may cause serious health problems. If you encourage her to get physical exercise every day, you will increase her brain capacity—and her life span.

8. Encourage outdoor play whenever you can.

Try to give your child time to play outdoors as often as possible. The rules of outdoor play are entirely different from those of indoor play, and spending time outside will amplify her sensory experiences and allow her to explore a wider range of behaviors. When she's playing in the yard, on the playground, or in the park, she can make more noise, be more physically active, do messy activities that aren't allowed at home or in school, and perform intriguing experiments with natural objects. And seeing trees, sunlight, puddles, streams, and live animals will expand her world and ignite her imagination.

9. Be playful in everyday life.

Your playfulness is contagious. If you make a funny face or sound while you're feeding your infant, she'll imitate you and make a funny face or sound. If you pretend a bar of soap can talk when you're giving your toddler a bath, your child will join right in on the fun. (*"Hi! My name is Slimy Soap. What's your name?"*) Turn mundane household chores into a game or contest, and you will lift your child's spirits and IQ. (*"Who can match up the pairs of socks the fastest?"*) Sing nonsense rhymes while you're cooking and ask your child to add every other line. (*"I love blue soup./Let's jump through a hoop."*) The more you play, the more resilient your child's brain will become and the easier it will be for her to learn.

10. Give your child a few minutes of undivided attention for play.

I know you're busy, busy, busy. But sit down and play with your child for a few minutes even if it means cutting corners on daily chores. Playing with your child will strengthen your relationship, build trust, keep you tuned in to her emotional life, and help her grow emotionally, intellectually, and socially.

Here are a few ways to play with your child:

- Sit on the floor in your child's room and act out a scene with dolls or action figures.

- Dress up in costumes or silly hats and make up a short play.

- Create a new recipe and try it out.

- Perform an experiment in the kitchen sink with food coloring and cold cereal.

- Decorate a dollhouse.

- Study maps and plan a real or imaginary trip.

- Draw a new superhero on poster paper (*"Klutzy Man—the guy with four left feet"*).

- Think up or draw wacky inventions (a flying garbage pail, motorized sneakers).

- Play card games, board games, chess, or checkers.

11. Make sure caregivers encourage your child to engage in free play.

> ** *You don't want your child spending long hours in an overstructured environment where cleanliness is more important than creativity and fun.* **

It is vital that the other adults who care for your child in your home, at a daycare center, or nursery school also have a positive attitude about playfulness and creativity. You don't want your child spending long hours in an overstructured environment where cleanliness is more important than creativity and fun; nor do you want caregivers to park your child in front of a TV or computer. If your child repeatedly tells you she's bored, that may be a signal that she needs a richer environment where she can play more often and without restraint.

Chapter 4 Review

Main Points

- A child instinctively plays to learn and learns by playing: the more she plays, the more stimulation she gives her brain, and the smarter she gets.

- Every kind of play—including digital activities—can help your child build new skills. But free play is especially beneficial because it involves all five senses and stimulates neural wiring that runs from head to toe, thereby turning her whole body—not just her brain—into a vehicle for learning.

- Unstructured, three-dimensional play:

  - Stimulates new brain wiring.

  - Increases a child's ability to concentrate.

  - Expands her capacity to learn new skills.

  - Widens knowledge of the world.

  - Enhances problem-solving skills.

  - Fosters patience, creativity, curiosity, empathy, perseverance, and self-control; and reinforces an appetite for learning.

All of these things will make it easier for your child to become a lifelong reader and learner, increase her cognitive and emotional intelligence, and help her succeed in school and life.

Actions

▶ Childproof your home and equip it for nontech fun.

▶ After stopping your child from doing something unacceptable, look for a way to encourage the learning impulse.

▶ Use everyday objects as toys.

▶ Do not overschedule your child.

▶ Express admiration for your child's playfulness.

▶ Reinforce your child's habit of becoming engaged in activities.

▶ Encourage regular physical exercise.

▶ Encourage outdoor play whenever you can.

▶ Be playful in everyday life.

▶ Give your child a few minutes of undivided attention for play.

▶ Make sure caregivers encourage your child's playfulness.

Chapter 5

Step Three:
Read to Your Child and Expand How, When, and What You Read Aloud

You've watched the scene in dozens of Hollywood movies: A parent sits on the edge of the bed, reads a fairytale to his darling little child, kisses him good night, and tiptoes out of the room. The scene is heartwarming and charming, but it has brainwashed millions of parents to think that reading aloud means reading a kiddy book to a silent toddler at bedtime.

Don't misunderstand: There's nothing wrong with reading to your toddler when you tuck him in at night. On the contrary, it's a wonderful habit to have. In the 1980s, when the U.S. Department of Education asked a panel of experts to analyze the results of ten thousand reading research projects, the panel reported that reading aloud is the "single most important activity for eventual success in reading." Reading aloud is so effective, in fact, that the panel went on to say that parents should continue reading aloud even after their children learn to read.

But you can increase your child's pleasure and provide him with a life-changing experience if you expand how, when, and what you read to him. Changing your approach to reading aloud will increase his:

- appetite for books and reading

- IQ (intellectual intelligence) and EQ (emotional intelligence)

- reading ability

- vocabulary

- abstract thinking skills

- ability to do well in school

- knowledge of the world

- capacity for empathy

- creativity

- emotional bond with you

By making a few small changes in your read-aloud habits—which won't cost you extra time—you will help your child grow emotionally, intellectually, and socially; increase the fun of reading; and strengthen your relationship with him. It's a win-win situation for both of you.

How to Read to Your Child

Let's start with the way you read aloud: When your child sits quietly and listens to you read, he benefits from hearing the steady flow of words. However, since you are doing all the talking, you have no way of knowing what he's really getting out of the experience. Is he listening or daydreaming? Is he following the plot or is he confused? Does he grasp the motivations of the characters? Does he comprehend new vocabulary words? Does he get the meaning of the illustrations?

But if you periodically stop and interact with him about what you are reading, you will make the experience deeper and more pleasurable. You might pause to make a comment about an illustration, ask a question, have a brief chat about a character, clarify the plot, explain the meaning of a word, or connect something in the story to your child's life. In other words, use the book as a starting point for a conversation about anything that interests either of you. And let your child direct the conversation so he does most of the talking and you become his audience.

You can read interactively whether you're reading a picture book to your infant or toddler or a novel to an older child who knows how to read. In both instances, your goal is the same: to engage your child in the material so he thinks about it, feels it, and talks about it.

Here is what happens when you turn your monologue into a dialogue:

- When you chat about the material, your child hears and uses a variety of words.

- When you ask questions that require thought, he practices his abstract thinking skills, which will make it easier for him to function in school where he will be expected to do a lot of abstract thinking.

- When you explain the meaning of words, his vocabulary grows.

- When you connect the story or book or picture to his daily life, his knowledge of the world expands, his understanding of human nature deepens, and he develops a capacity for empathy.

- When you analyze the meaning of an illustration, he learns how to make inferences—that is, to "read between the lines."

- When you express your curiosity about something, his own natural curiosity is ignited and reinforced.

- When you share your thoughts and feelings, you connect with him on an emotional level.

Reading interactively helps you stay close.

" Reading interactively is an easy way to stay emotionally close to your child without infringing on his privacy— or yours."

You live in the same house as your child, but that doesn't mean you always have entrance into his inner life, especially if he goes to school all day. If you ask him a direct question (*"How was school today?"*), he may give you a monosyllabic answer (*"Good"* or *"Bad"*). If he does give you a bit of information and you ask for details, he may clam up. In reverse, your child may not know much about the issues and problems you grapple with on a daily basis. While a measure of privacy is important for both of you, you don't want to get so out of touch that you end up being familiar-looking strangers who happen to live at the same address.

Reading interactively is an easy way to stay emotionally close to your child without infringing on his privacy—or yours. When you travel through a book together, you meet new people and experience a wide assortment of emotions. Talking about these "trips" with your child gives him a comfortable way to express his fears, hopes, dreams, and problems—and it gives you insight into his emotional life. For example, if he's upset about how a friend has been treating him but doesn't want to be a tattletale by telling you about the situation, he may be willing to talk about it if a similar dynamic crops up in a book you're reading together. Sharing a book invites a safe level of intimacy and openness that isn't always possible in other settings.

In reverse, sharing books gives you a comfortable way to express emotions and ideas to your child while his character is taking shape. I'm not referring to the standard behavioral admonishments we all offer our children—be nice, be neat, be polite, etc. I'm talking about the values that inform your choices and behavior—your philosophy of life. For example, if you think perseverance is the key to being successful, you can talk about this idea with your toddler when you're reading

The Little Engine That Could. You can do the same with your eight-year-old when the two of you meet Reepicheep, the brave and determined little mouse in the *Narnia* series, or with your twelve-year-old when you read about Bilbo's determination to complete his quest in *The Hobbit.* By weaving your beliefs into literary conversations, you can give your child a moral and social framework that makes it easier for him to understand what makes you tick. It also gives your child the vocabulary to start building his own standard of ethics.

In my own case, reading books aloud to my children before and after they learned to read helped me create a special bond with them that has lasted well beyond their childhoods. For example, today if I ask my adult children whether a specific piece of clothing I'm wearing looks ridiculous, they invariably answer, *"They'll laugh,"* a throwback line from *Ira Sleeps Over,* a picture book we read decades ago. If I'm grumpy, they teasingly refer to me as Ma Baxter, after the life-toughened mom in *The Yearling.* When I offer medical advice, they call me Nurse Ratched, after the character from the adult novel *One Flew Over the Cuckoo's Nest.* When I want to describe someone who is kind to everyone except himself, I only have to say he's like Sully, the protagonist of Richard Russo's novel, *Nobody's Fool,* and they know exactly what I mean. Characters we met in books and talked about when they were children are still part of the fabric of our relationship.

In the movie classic *Casablanca,* Humphrey Bogart famously says to Ingrid Bergman, "We'll always have Paris." If you travel through books with your child, the two of you will share a literary world and dozens of "friends" even after he becomes an adult—and nothing will erase those memories.

❝ *If you travel through books with your child, the two of you will share a literary world and dozens of "friends" even after he becomes an adult—and nothing will erase those memories.* ❞

Remember: Pleasure is the goal.

Although it's fruitful to pause periodically and chat about what you're reading, your child's enjoyment is always your first order of business so that he associates reading with pleasure. Don't try to turn every interchange into an educational moment. If you constantly interrupt the flow of a story by making comments or peppering him with questions, you'll ruin the fun and quash his appetite for reading.

Pay attention to your child's cues. If he gets restless while you're reading to him, offer to read something else or stop reading. If a particular passage bores him (my kids hated descriptions of nature, which we referred to as flora and fauna), skip it and move on. If your child is anxious to hear how a suspenseful story ends, read it without stopping. If he wants to keep his hands busy while he's listening, let him draw, color, or play quietly with a toy or doll while you're reading. If he wants to read the same book over and over, that's fine, too—even if you're bored with it, he's not. If he gets more involved in playing than listening, put the book down and don't make him feel guilty. He's not in school, and you're not his teacher. His pleasure trumps all other considerations.

One last point: When you read interactively with your child, you end up reading fewer pages at a time than you would if you read the material straight through. But it's more important to engage your child in the reading experience than it is to complete a specific number of pages or books. The goal is not to cross a finish line, but to help your child grow. Give him as much time as he wants to ask questions and make comments. The more he explores ideas and feelings, the richer the experience will be for him.

How to Engage Your Child in Reading Material

1. **Make a comment or ask a question about an illustration:**
   "See the three white rabbits hiding behind the bushes? Let's count them. One, two, three rabbits."
   "Why do you think the moose is frowning in that picture?"

2. **Clarify the plot:**
   "Bobby is moping around the house because his best friend moved away, and he's lonely."
   "Sara is chasing the puppy, and her little brother is chasing her."

3. **Connect events and characters in the book to real life:**
   "How did you feel when your favorite stuffed animal fell apart?"
   "Remember when we got so lost that we ended up in the wrong town?"

4. **Ask thought-provoking questions that can't be answered with a "yes" or "no":**
   "Why do you think Pete is so unhappy about going to a new school?"
   "What would you do if you got locked in the museum?"

5. Express your curiosity:

"Do you think baby birds know how to fly when they're born?"

"I wonder why zebras aren't domesticated, even though they look like striped horses?"

6. Encourage your child's curiosity:

"That's a great question. Let's try to find out where snakes go in the winter."

"Why do you think pepper makes us sneeze?"

7. Ask your child to make inferences about the illustrations, plot, or characters:

"Why is the king frowning at the court jester?"

"How do you think the boys feel about being lost in the cave?"

8. Ask your child to make predictions about the plot:

"What's going to happen if the puppy steals the bone from the big dog?"

"Do you think the prince will decide to stay in the wizard's castle or go home?"

9. Ask for your child's opinion about an aspect of the story:

"How could William help his pal get out of that jam?"

"Do you think the racecar driver should stay in the race or drop out?"

10. Discuss the personalities and motivations of characters:

"Why do you think the new girl in the class is acting so snooty?"

"Was the store owner trying to make a fast buck, or did he genuinely want to help Jack?"

11. Repeat your child's answers to questions and expand them:

"I agree the goose looks ridiculous in the Santa costume, but he looked even sillier dressed as a vampire."

"Yes, I agree the detective seems pretty stupid. But maybe he's just putting on an act to fool people."

12. Express your personal values and beliefs through reading material:

"The Sneetches feel a lot of pressure to copy what their friends are doing. But it's silly to copy everyone else. You have to follow your own rules."

"Huck was an instinctively moral person, so he decided to violate the law and help the slave Jim escape. Sometimes you have to follow your own conscience."

When to Read to Your Child

It's wonderful to be able to read to your child for a large chunk of time before he goes to sleep—a sweet way to end the day. I enjoyed this ritual enormously and got my kids thoroughly addicted to it. But adult life is complicated and demanding, and you may not always have the time, energy, or inclination to read aloud in the evening. Or maybe your work or social schedule prevents you from being home at your child's bedtime. Or maybe you *do* read to your child at night but want to increase his exposure to reading. In any case, you don't have to limit yourself to single daily read-aloud sessions—or restrict reading sessions to the evening. You can also give your child short reading snacks at other times in the day by following the Boy Scout motto: Be prepared.

Keep read-aloud books handy everywhere in your house—in the kitchen, bedrooms, bathroom, living room—so they are nearby if an opportunity to read suddenly arises. Keep a little book or a few pages of reading material in your purse or brief-case, coat pocket, car, and stroller so you can read when you have a few moments between activities.

You can grab a book and read to your infant for two minutes when he's snuggled on your lap, lying in his crib, sitting on the floor sucking on a bottle, or eating a meal. Read to your toddler while he's taking a bath or eating finger food. Read to your kindergartner while you're on the bus or train or are waiting for a slice of pizza at a deli. Read to your third grader while you're in the car waiting to pick up his sibling from school or a party. Read to your sixth grader when you're sitting in a doctor's office. These short spans of time will add up. The more you read to your child, the better off he will be.

I managed to tuck a bit of extra reading into my children's day by stuffing a book into my coat pocket when I shepherded them down to our building's lobby in the mornings and waited for the school bus to arrive. Sometimes the boys felt like running around like monkeys, or we were too sleepy or grumpy to read. But on many mornings, we squeezed together on a bench and read until the bus appeared. It often came right away, but on rainy and snowy days it might be ten or fifteen minutes late. However long the extra dollop of reading pleasure lasted, it was a great way for the children to kick off their busy school day—and it exposed them to thousands of words over the course of grade school.

It's tempting to use stray moments to check messages, send emails, talk to friends and business associates, or play games on your phone. But remember: You have the rest of your life to talk on the phone, but only one shot at raising your child. Once he grows up, you won't be able to go back in time and redo his childhood.

Enlist substitute readers to read aloud.

You don't have to be the only one who reads to your child. Ask other people to pitch in—your child's older siblings, grand-parents, aunts, uncles, cousins, family friends, and caregivers. Or hire a young neighborhood child to come over and spend a few minutes reading to your child while you're in the house doing chores or entertaining friends.

Explain the importance of reading aloud to your assistant readers so they understand how much they are helping your child. If your child attends a day care center or nursery school, make sure the teacher or assistant spends time reading at some point in the day. Remember that children learn to talk and read by connecting with other people and sharing words—not by watching "educational programs" on TV or the computer.

Supplement human readers with technology.

Now that videos are so popular, it's easy to forget that children love to hear stories as well as see them. An audiobook or podcast won't fully replace a human reader. Machines can't cuddle, ask thought-provoking questions, chat, or explain the meaning of words. But just listening to books, stories, and other programs will entertain your child, expose him to thousands of new words, increase his language processing skills, expand his vocabulary, and reinforce the pleasure of reading.

Start your child off by listening with him while he's drinking a bottle, playing quietly with dolls or toys, drawing and coloring, or riding in the car with you. If the two of you share this pleasure often enough, he will get into the habit of listening to stories whether or not you are in the room.

You can download listening material from the Internet, borrow CDs from your local library, or buy CDs online, at bookstores, flea markets, community bazaars, and street fairs (Learning Ally, which was formerly known as Recording for the Blind and Dyslexic, is a national, nonprofit organization that has an enormous online library of audio material).

Keep audio equipment in your child's bedroom or in an accessible place in your home. Take your equipment and listening material along when you travel in a car, plane, bus, or train. The more your child listens to words, the easier it will be for him to become a reader.

> *Start your child off by listening with him. If you share this pleasure often enough, he will get into the habit of listening to stories whether or not you are in the room.*"

Weave reading into your child's everyday life.

Your child knows that people need to eat to keep their bodies strong and healthy. Make sure he also knows that people need to read to keep their minds strong and healthy. It's not sufficient to tell your child *reading is good for you* and leave it at that. You need to reinforce the vital importance of reading, which you can do in four ways.

1 *Fill your house with books and other reading materials.*

2 *Model the behavior of a happy reader by reading books, e-books, magazines, and newspapers yourself.*

3 *Take your child to the library or bookstore as often as possible (studies show that children who become readers are taken to the library on a regular basis).*

4 *Encourage your child to satisfy his natural curiosity by reading.*

For example, if your child is home from school in February on Lincoln's birthday and asks a question about the president, get a book about Lincoln from a library or bookstore, or download material from the Internet and read part or all of it out loud. If your child is curious about why onions make his eyes sting with tears, help him look up the answer in a science book or online and read the information to him. If he wonders how planes can stay up in the air, find a biography of the Wright brothers and read some or all of it aloud. On religious holidays, get a book about a great religious figure and read it to him. If your child asks the meaning of a word, help him look it up in the dictionary or on an e-reader and read the definition out loud.

If reading is a part of your child's daily life, he will develop the habit of using books for pleasure and information, and books will nourish his heart, mind, and soul.

What to Read to Your Child— Expand the Horizons

Thousands of fabulous books have been written specifically for children. But children's literature isn't the only kind of material you can read aloud. Your child is massively curious about the world and understands many more words than he can read (his reading skills won't catch up to his listening skills until around eighth grade). Material written for adults often contains more varied information, more complex syntax, and a greater range of vocabulary than is commonly found in children's literature. If you expand your choice of reading matter, you will expand your child's world and whet his appetite for reading and learning.

When you are reading anything—a book, newspaper, magazine, advertisement, or email—keep your eyes peeled for a sentence, paragraph, or page you think your child might enjoy. It might be a news article about ridiculous hats worn at a royal wedding, a profile of a sports hero, a scorching attack on a political candidate, a witty email from a friend, a vivid description of a criminal in a mystery, or even an obituary (I know this last suggestion sounds macabre, but obituaries are minibiographies, and they are often fascinating. Just don't tell your child the person has died if you don't want to). Either rip it out of the newspaper or magazine, or mark the place in the book and put it away for future use. Then read it to your child at a meal, while you're standing on line at the grocery store, or when you're sitting in a restaurant waiting for your burgers and fries. Or drift into his room and say, *"Hey, listen to this description of wild camels in Australia who attacked air conditioners in search of drinking water."* (A real event, by the way.)

Here's an example: When I was reading *Iron and Silk*, Mark Salzman's memoir about teaching English and studying martial arts in China in the 1980s, I came across a riveting description of a fierce martial arts teacher with an "iron fist." Since my then eight-year-old dyslexic son was studying karate, I read the short paragraph to him. He was so intrigued that he asked me to read a little more about the man. And more. Then he asked me to go back and start at the beginning of the book—which I did, skipping difficult or inappropriate sections.

What did my son get from this listening experience? Exposure to dozens of interesting new words such as sheepish, hindered, austere, and mediocre; an introduction to Chinese customs, culture, culinary habits, and politics; lessons about the effect that small gestures of kindness can have on people; and a renewed desire to learn how to read well despite the fact that he was struggling with reading in school.

❝ Don't worry about the reading level of a book. Experiment with anything you think your child might enjoy.❞

Here's another example: My children and I were gripped by the subject of bullies in literature—or rather, by the question of how a gentle person can defend himself and protect others against bullies. The issue cropped up in several books we read together, such as C. S. Lewis's *The Lion, the Witch and the Wardrobe* and Brian Jacques's *Redwall*. So when I came across a battered copy of the adult novel *Shane* by Jack Schaefer at a flea market, I decided to read it to the boys. The simply written novel is about a retired gunfighter who tries to avoid violence but has to strap his guns back on when bullies threaten his friends. As we read the book, we talked about our own experiences with bullies, the importance of coming to the defense of others who are being bullied, and the physical and mental courage it takes to confront bullies. The boys enjoyed the book so much that when I came across an audiotape version, I bought it and gave it to them to listen to before they fell asleep at night. Then I rented the classic 1953 movie version starring Alan Ladd with a screenplay by A. B. Guthrie, Jr., and we enjoyed watching it together and comparing it to the book. When they each learned how to read, they reread it on their own. Recently, the same dog-eared copy turned up in my house, and I plan to reread it one of these days myself. Unless, of course, one of my sons comes for a visit, spots it on my nightstand, and makes off with it before I get to it.

Don't worry about the reading level of a book. Experiment with anything you think your child might enjoy. If either of you finds a book boring or incomprehensible, ditch it and read something else. No harm done.

Remember that certain classics like George Orwell's *Animal Farm* and Mark Twain's *The Adventures of Tom Sawyer* use relatively simple language but contain complex ideas. Books like these can be read to a little child as well as a teenager, and both will enjoy the experience. Even adult books that may not be appropriate for children in their entirety can be mined for passages that are touching, gripping, or fascinating. For example, a child wouldn't enjoy hearing all of Cervantes's epic novel *Don Quixote*, but several slapstick scenes are very funny. Adult mysteries are too scary to read to a young child, but he might enjoy hearing a vivid description of a quirky character.

Age Differences Between Children Don't Matter

Good parenting isn't about perfection. It's about doing the best you can with imperfect circumstances."

Three Helpful Ideas to Share with Your Child

In a perfect world, you would have time to read to each of your children separately every day. But modern life doesn't permit this luxury. In fact, you may find it a stretch to do any reading at all. But good parenting isn't about perfection. It's about doing the best you can with imperfect circumstances. So don't give up the idea of reading aloud even if you have very little time and several children. You can read to all of them at once despite their age differences.

I've thought about this a lot because my own children are spread far apart in age (the older boys were seven and eleven when their younger brother was born). I read aloud to them as often as I could, partly because I love to read and they all loved being read to, and partly because I wanted to share my love of reading. But since I was often with two—if not all three—boys, I had to figure out how to make the experience appealing to all of them at once.

As a writer and former English teacher, I had the advantage of knowing three important things about books, which I explained to my children:

① *Good writing is good writing no matter what form it takes.*

② *An interesting idea is worth exploring.*

③ *Books are toys for the mind that can be used in any number of ways.*

1. Good writing is good writing.

From the start, I made it abundantly clear that good writing can be found in many forms—children's picture books, adult novels, comics, brochures, magazines, and even instruction manuals. As a result, the older boys weren't ashamed of enjoying their little brother's picture books. In our house, we weren't snooty about "baby" books or comics; we disdained lousy writing that was boring, shallow, clichéd, or predictable. As far as we were concerned, good books were those we enjoyed. Bad books were those we disliked (this didn't eliminate the possibility that a "bad" book might become more appealing in the future. It just meant we didn't like it at that moment).

The fact that my older children weren't ashamed of enjoying material meant for younger children and my youngest son was used to listening to "big boy" content gave me license to read a wide range of things to them—books written for small children, new readers, and sophisticated readers, as well as sections of novels written for adults. How did I keep the older boys interested in picture books and the toddler interested in novels? By reading interactively—that is, by periodically stopping to make a comment about an illustration, talk about a character, discuss an aspect of the plot, or explore a gripping or silly idea. Naturally, my conversations with my toddler or new reader were very different from my interactions with the older children. But no matter the level of the book, my conversations with each of my children would be genuine and age appropriate.

2. An interesting idea is worth exploring.

When an interesting idea cropped up in a book, I encouraged the boys to think about, talk about, and explore it. For example, when I read Dr. Seuss's picture book, *I Had Trouble in Getting to Solla Sollew*, to all three boys at once, I read a page or two, then paused to point out a funny illustration to my toddler and talk about the concept behind the drawing with the older children.

The book is about a creature who leaves home to escape from problems but is plagued by new problems as he makes his way to Solla Sollew, "Where they never have troubles! At least, very few." After several misadventures, the protagonist realizes that problems exist everywhere and decides to return home. He arms himself with a bat and proclaims: "Now my troubles are going to have trouble with me." The boys all enjoyed looking at the wacky illustrations, and the serious ideas underlying the fable gave us many things to chat about: courage, cowardice, self-protectiveness, the search for perfection, and the quirks of fate that happen to everybody.

On the other hand, when I read an illustrated edition of *The Hobbit* to my older children, I sat my younger son on my lap, read a few pages, and stopped to explain a new word, point out something interesting about an illustration, or explain part of the plot to the toddler. He was too young to understand the whole story, but he enjoyed being physically close to me and spending time with his older brothers. He was also mesmerized by the colorful, intricate illustrations of hobbits and other creatures. When he got restless, I'd distract him with a toy or snack and continue reading. When his interruptions became annoyingly frequent, I'd stop. But even if we managed to get in only a few minutes of reading time, we all thought it was worth the effort.

3. Books are toys for the mind that can be used in a variety of ways.

To keep my older children amused when I read picture books to their little brother, I'd jazz up the reading experience in a few different ways. I might ask one of the older boys to do the reading or suggest that they both take turns. Or I'd flip to the last page of the book and ask them to make up a whole new story based on the reverse order of the illustrations. Or I'd start reading in a foreign or silly accent and ask the older children to read using that same accent or their own nutty accent. As soon as they got bored, I'd stop and we'd find something else to do separately or as a group.

Share Your Work, Hobbies, and Passions with Your Child

Reading material aloud that relates to your job or favorite hobby is a great way to bond with your child. I'm not suggesting that you read textbooks or how-to manuals out loud. But if you share tidbits of things that interest you, you'll give him some understanding of who you are, what you think about, and what you do for a living or for recreation.

> **❝ A passion for reading isn't contagious; it's an acquired habit. I know plenty of adults who love to read but have children who never open a book.❞**

If you're a lawyer or are passionate about politics, read parts of newspaper articles or editorials about hot-button issues such as immigration, abortion, or affirmative action and talk about these things with your child. If you're a professional chef or enjoy cooking, read restaurant reviews or unusual recipes out loud. If you're a bird watcher, read aloud interesting articles from a magazine like *National Geographic* or read a few paragraphs about birds from Jonathan Franzen's novel *Freedom*. If you're a teacher, read the uplifting note you recently received from a former student.

A passion for reading isn't contagious—it's an acquired habit. I know plenty of adults who love to read but have children who never open a book. While it's important to be a role model for your child and fill your home with books, you also need to reinforce your child's natural enjoyment of books by sharing intriguing and amusing content while he's learning to read. If you share your zest for reading with him, he will also approach books with zest and become a lifelong reader.

Chapter 5 Review

Main Points

- You can increase your child's pleasure and provide him with a life-changing experience if you expand how, when, and what you read to him. Changing your approach to reading aloud will increase his:

  - appetite for books and reading

  - IQ (intellectual intelligence) and EQ (emotional intelligence)

  - reading ability

  - vocabulary

  - abstract thinking skills

  - ability to do well in school

  - knowledge of the world

  - capacity for empathy

  - creativity

  - emotional bond with you

- While reading aloud, if you periodically stop and engage with your child about what you've been reading, you will make the experience deeper and more pleasurable.

- Sharing books is an easy way to stay emotionally close to your child without infringing on his privacy—or yours.

- Although it's fruitful to pause periodically and chat about what you're reading, your child's enjoyment is always your first order of business. Don't try to turn every interchange into an "educational moment." If you constantly interrupt the flow of a story by making comments or peppering him with questions, you'll ruin the fun and quash his appetite for reading.

- Age differences between children don't matter. Don't give up the idea of reading aloud even if you have very little time and several children. You can read to all of them at once despite their age differences.

- Three important ideas about books to share with your children:

  - Good writing is good writing no matter what form it takes.

  - An interesting idea is worth exploring.

  - Books are toys for the mind that can be used in any number of ways.

- Material written for adults often contains more varied information, more complex syntax, and a greater range of vocabulary words than is commonly found in children's literature. If you widen your choice of reading matter, you will help your child grow linguistically, intellectually, and emotionally, and whet his appetite for reading and learning.

Actions

▶ When reading out loud, pause to make a comment about an illustration, ask a question, have a brief chat about a character, clarify the plot, explain the meaning of a word, or connect something in the story to your child's life. Use the book as a springboard for conversations about anything that interests either of you.

▶ Ask thought-provoking questions that can't be answered with a yes or no.

▶ Encourage your child's curiosity and express your own.

▶ Ask your child to make inferences about the illustrations, plot, or characters; make predictions about the plot; or share his opinion about an aspect of the story.

▶ Discuss the personalities and motivations of the characters.

▶ Express your personal values and beliefs through reading material.

▶ Enlist substitute readers to read aloud to your child.

▶ Supplement human readers with audio technology.

▶ Weave reading into your child's everyday life.

▶ Share your work, hobbies, and passions with your child.

....

▶ Take your child to the library as often as possible.

....

Chapter 6

Step Four:
Support and Motivate
Your New Reader

Imagine coming home from a long day of work and having to sit down and practice reading Sanskrit for half an hour and you'll get a sense of how your new reader feels about opening her reading book every night.

Yet the old adage, "practice makes perfect," is especially applicable to reading. Reading is learned in stages, and each new stage is built upon skills learned at a previous stage. The only way your child will master new skills and progress to the next reading level is by practicing at home every day.

But practicing is very hard work for your beginner, especially after a full day at school. Because she has to spend so much mental effort on sounding out words, she can't focus on or enjoy the story, so reading feels like a chore. She'd much rather watch TV or play video games, or do almost anything except open a book.

Warning: This is a critical time in your child's life.

Your new reader is at a momentous crossroads. But family life is so hectic and demanding and reading is such a slow, quiet process that you may not realize how vulnerable she is right now—or understand that her future is at stake (the situation always reminds me of the line spoken by Miss Alma in Tennessee Williams's play *The Eccentricities of a Nightingale:* "How gently a failure can happen!"). So let me lay it out for you:

If your child becomes a skilled, passionate reader by the end of grade school, she is likely to feel relaxed and confident in the classroom, view herself as a smart person, become an academic success, have time for friends and extracurricular activities, enjoy school, and stay in school long enough to become well educated. This will afford her a wide choice of personal and professional options in life.

Conversely, if she gets snagged at a basic skill level in the early grades and remains a weak reader, her self-esteem will be battered, books will become enemies, she will be a poor or mediocre student, feel anxious and frustrated in the classroom, leave school as soon as she can, and end up with fewer choices. Thus her life will spin off in an entirely different direction.

I'm not claiming that becoming an excellent reader will guarantee your child health, happiness, and success. The world is far too unpredictable for guarantees. But becoming a skilled reader will have a beneficial effect on her personality, make it easier for her to deal with misfortune and accidents of fate, and give her a better shot at leading a satisfying and productive life.

It's Easier Than You Think to Support a New Reader

Contrary to the commonly held belief that it's "impossible" to raise readers, helping your child become an avid reader isn't difficult or time consuming. It won't entail pushing, pressuring, teaching, tutoring, banning technology, or banishing her to her room for long, lonely practice sessions. It is mostly a question of changing your attitude about reading and approaching the subject in a loving and positive way ("Rah, rah!" instead of "Nag, nag!").

Keep in mind that there is a tremendous emotional component to becoming a reader. Studies show that when a child associates learning with pleasure, her body releases chemicals that help her brain operate on an optimal level. She becomes more engaged and more motivated in the learning process.

Your goal is to help your child get over the tough hurdle of the beginner stage of reading that virtually everyone confronts, so she develops enough skills to enjoy reading. Once she thinks of reading as a treat—not a treatment—she will read often. The more she reads, the better she will get at it and the easier and more enjoyable it will become.

> *Studies show that when a child associates learning with pleasure, her body releases chemicals that help her brain operate on an optimal level."*

You can turn your new reader into a lifelong reader by doing three things:

1 *Reinforce her natural appetite for books while she's learning to read.*

2 *Fuel her enthusiasm for reading so she is motivated to become a reader.*

3 *Make it as easy as possible for her to practice reading at home.*

In this chapter, I'll share a "bag of tricks" that will make it simple for you to accomplish your goal. But before I get into specifics, I want to explain why your support will have such a huge impact on your child's reading future.

How a Child Learns to Read

Reading looks easy, but neurobiologists tell us it is one of the most complex and challenging cognitive activities humans endeavor to do. Reading uses both hemispheres of the brain and involves memory, experience, imagination, language and motor skills, visual perception, and executive functions, such as the ability to ignore distractions and focus on a task until completion.

In addition to being an enormously complicated mental under-taking, reading is also a relatively new activity for humans: We've been on the planet for about two hundred thousand years but have only been reading for about five thousand. So we are not naturally wired for reading the way we are naturally wired for other activities such as seeing, hearing, and moving our arms and legs. This is why a child needs formal reading lessons in school.

To become a reader, a child must learn how to convert brain wiring meant for other purposes and use it to connect little black squiggles on a page with alphabetic letters, connect letters with sounds, connect sounds with words, connect words with meaning, and store meaning in memory. This multistep process is so demanding that it stimulates the brain to develop new wiring and grow in capacity. Reading literally turns a child into a "brainier" person.

The brain uses two separate neural pathways when a child is learning to read. The slower pathway is used during the beginning stage when a new reader painstakingly sounds out words letter-by-letter and syllable-by-syllable. Then once she masters the different steps involved in sounding out words, her brain switches over to a second set of interconnected wires that can process this information almost instantaneously. This high-speed wiring allows a skilled reader to look at a word, identify its separate sounds, retrieve its meaning, and store it in her memory so quickly that reading seems to happen automatically. It is this "reading fluency" that turns reading into a pleasurable experience.

A small percentage of children embrace reading at an early age and become fluent quite rapidly (it's similar to children who take to water right away and learn to swim soon after they jump into a pool or lake). But most children need years of instruction and practice to make this leap. And unfortunately, most children never get beyond the early stages of the reading process. They get snagged at a beginner stage (for a variety of reasons that I'll discuss in the next chapter); continue to be slow, plodding readers all through school; and shun books and reading ever after.

During this beginning stage, your child may say she "doesn't like" reading. It's important to understand that her complaint has nothing to do with competition from technology or her particular personality or temperament. It stems entirely from the fact that sounding out words and building reading skills are still very hard work for her.

Just saying to her, *"Reading is fun!"* won't be effective, because reading isn't fun for her at this point, and nothing you say can change that. Reading will only become fun if she becomes fluent—that is, learns to read so quickly, easily, and accurately that reading feels effortless.

Effortless Reading: The Most Important Reading Skill You've Never Heard Of

Effortless reading—the ability to glance at a word and decipher it in a flash—is the single most important skill your child will be taught in grade school. Why? Because it will turn reading from a taxing chore into a delight, and turn your child from someone who knows how to read into someone who loves to read. And this will change her life.

But teachers cannot do the whole job of turning your child into an effortless reader. They need you as their partner.

Teachers will introduce new reading skills in the classroom and may provide some practice time during the school day. Many schools employ reading programs known by various names: DEAR (Drop Everything And Read), DIRT (Daily Individual Reading Time), SQUIRT (Sustained Quiet Uninterrupted Reading Time), and VFR (Voluntary Free Reading). But this won't be enough practice for your child to become fluent. She needs to practice reading at home on a regular basis. Since teachers cannot come home with your child, it is your job to make sure your child practices at home.

You are the only one who can protect your child from the disastrous cycle that will prevent her from becoming a skilled reader. Without your support, here is what can happen:

Because she is tired when she comes home from school, she won't feel like reading. The less she reads, the less she improves. The less she improves, the less she will want to read and the less likely she will become an expert reader. She will get stuck at a beginner skill level in grade school, continue to find reading an unpleasant task all through school, and graduate with a lifelong aversion to books and reading.

How can you possibly motivate your child to sit down and practice reading when the two of you are so busy and tired in the evening? Happily, you already know the answer. In fact, you are an expert at motivating your child because you've done it many times before.

The Familiar Method of Support

Whenever you've helped your child learn a new recreational skill—to swim, skate, bike, bake, build model airplanes, fly a kite, repair old cars—you instinctively behaved in a certain way. Let's use biking as an example and see what you did when you taught her how to ride a bike.

You started by giving your toddler a small plastic motorcycle or a little tricycle because you knew she'd enjoy riding and would benefit from the exercise. When she got a bit older, you gave her a slightly larger vehicle. Then you gave her a two-wheeler with training wheels. When she was old enough to learn to ride the two-wheeler, you removed the extra wheels and explained a few things to her. You told her that staying balanced would be difficult at first but would get easier and easier with practice, and would eventually become automatic. You also told her that once she became a rider, she'd enjoy biking for the rest of her life.

Then you helped her onto the bike and held the seat to prevent her from falling and getting hurt. You ran alongside while she practiced, praised her to build her confidence, and cheered her on so she wouldn't get frustrated and demoralized. As her skill and self-confidence increased, you let go of her seat for longer and longer periods but stayed close by in case she lost her balance. After she learned to stay balanced while pedaling, steering, and braking, she could ride on her own—and both of you were thrilled.

The process of learning to ride a bike can be broken into four stages:

- **Stage 1:** You give your child age-appropriate vehicles so she can have fun and develop a strong, healthy body.

- **Stage 2:** When she's old enough for a two-wheeler, you explain that riding is difficult at first but will get easier with practice and eventually become automatic. You also coach her by explaining that the hard work of practicing will pay off because she'll enjoy biking for the rest of her life.

- **Stage 3:** You reduce her anxiety and minimize the boredom and frustration by cheering her on and praising her for practicing.

- **Stage 4:** When she develops enough skill to ride on her own, she loves riding.

Now let's substitute reading for biking:

- **Stage 1:** You introduce your young child to letters, words, and books so she can have fun and develop a strong, healthy mind.

- **Stage 2:** When she's old enough to learn to read, you explain that reading is difficult at first but will get easier with practice and eventually become automatic. You also make it clear that the hard work of practicing will pay off because she'll enjoy reading for the rest of her life.

- **Stage 3:** You reduce her anxiety and minimize the boredom and frustration by cheering her on and praising her for practicing.

- **Stage 4:** When she develops enough skill to read on her own, she loves reading.

Notice that you shared the fun of biking early in your child's life and acted as her cheerleader and supporter from the time she got her first tricycle until she learned to ride a two-wheeler. You motivated her to want to learn to ride and stayed close to her while she was a beginner. You neither pushed nor berated her during the learning stage. You worked with her to accomplish this goal. And you assumed she would learn to ride—and would enjoy riding when she could do it easily.

If you behave this same way when your child is learning to read, I promise you she will become a reader.

All Types of Children Can Become Excellent, Avid Readers

Despite what you've heard, it makes no difference whether your child is naturally sedentary or active and athletic. Nor does it matter whether she's a whiz kid who picks up reading quickly or has a reading glitch that makes reading a struggle. Studies show that all children can become readers if they get adequate instruction in school and adequate support and encouragement at home.

Below are nine specific ways to help your child master this vital skill. You'll be delighted to know that only two of my nine suggestions—reading aloud and oral guided reading—require your undivided attention (and as you will see below, you can even cut corners on these activities to make them more doable when you're super busy). The other seven suggestions only involve changing your approach to reading—something that will not cost you any extra time.

Studies show that all children can become readers if they get adequate instruction in school and adequate support and encouragement at home."

Easy Ways to Support Your New Reader

1. Bolster your child's enthusiasm for reading.

You need to share a few key ideas with your child before and while she is learning to read—not by mentioning them once or twice, but by telling her these things over and over again:

- Reading is the single most important skill she will learn in elementary school.

- Learning to read well will make her life in school—and as an adult—easier and more enjoyable.

- You are on her team. You are her advocate and supporter, not her adversary and critic.

- Reading is difficult at first, but it gets easier with practice and eventually becomes effortless.

- *When* she learns to read isn't important; what matters is that she learns to read well enough to *enjoy* reading.

- Practicing is hard work, but you will do everything you can to make her practice sessions as comfortable and pleasant as possible.

2. Continue to read aloud even after your child learns to read.

> **If you continue to read aloud to your child through the grades and she continues to enjoy books, she will want to become a better and better reader and will be willing to put in the effort to attain that goal."**

When your child was an infant and toddler, she loved looking at picture books and listening to you read aloud. But you need to reinforce the pleasure of books and reading while she's learning to read, or she may gradually begin to associate reading with homework and hard work and forget that books can be a source of entertainment. If you continue to read aloud to her through the grades and she continues to enjoy books, she will want to become a better and better reader, and be willing to put in the effort to attain that goal.

Read for long spans of time or give your child short reading "snacks" at stray moments in the day. Read a wide range of terrific material to her and don't restrict yourself to kiddy lit. Read sentences or paragraphs from newspaper or magazine articles, editorials and restaurant reviews, obituaries, novels and nonfiction books meant for adults, and comic books. Read anything your child enjoys. Reading to a child who has

already learned to read isn't spoiling or babying her. It is reinforcing the pleasure of reading, widening her vocabulary, and
increasing her knowledge of the world—all of which will help
her become an expert reader.

> ❝ *Reading to a child who has already learned*
> *to read isn't spoiling or babying her.*
> *It is reinforcing the pleasure of reading,*
> *widening her vocabulary, and increasing*
> *her knowledge of the world—all of which*
> *will help her become an expert reader.*❞

3. Ask your child to read out loud to you and give her feedback.

In the 1980s, when the National Reading Panel analyzed
research data on various teaching methods, they made an
important discovery: The programs that produce the largest
gains in fluency allow a child to read and reread a poem, paragraph, or passage in a story out loud with feedback and correction
as she reads. This method has several different names—guided
repeated oral reading, paired reading, shared reading, assisted
reading, or echo reading.

Guided reading is effective because a child needs to see a word
at least three to four times before she can decipher it quickly and
easily. When you give your child the chance to read the same
sentences out loud several times, she becomes so familiar with
those words that she then can recognize them in microseconds.

Pick a short poem, paragraph, or passage (approximately fifty to one hundred words) that you think your child will enjoy, or let her select something she wants to read (Shel Silverstein poems are great for this, by the way). If she chooses something she's already read, that's perfectly fine. She should be able to read the material so comfortably that you only need to correct her once or twice per page. If the poem or passage is too difficult, she'll get discouraged, frustrated, and bored.

You can make it easier for her to read the selection by reading it to her first so she can hear the correct pronunciation of words before she starts reading. Or you can let her read silently to herself so she becomes familiar with the passage before she reads it out loud. Or just ask her to read the poem or paragraph out loud three or four times until she can read it smoothly. Don't jump in and correct her immediately if she struggles with a word or mispronounces it. Give her a little time to figure it out, or ask her if that word makes sense in the sentence she's reading. But if she can't come up with the correct word in a few moments, tell it to her so she doesn't get discouraged.

Books of poems, picture books, and theater scripts are excellent to use for practice. You can download free theater scripts for children from the Internet and duplicate them so you can each have a copy. Four excellent sources of scripts for new readers can be found at:

Reader's Theater Editions
http://www.aaronshep.com/rt/RTE.html
Individual scripts for children 8–15

Children's Theatre Scripts and Plays Free from Whootie Owl
http://hazel.forest.net/whootie/script.html

Great plays from various parts of the world

Kidsinco
http://www.kidsinco.com/complete-list-of-playscripts
130 different play scripts, skits, and role plays for kids—there really is something for everyone

Poetry Teachers
http://www.poetryteachers.com/poetrytheater/theater.html
Terrific site with rhyming plays

You don't have to spend long stretches of time on guided reading, but it's a wonderful investment and has a big payoff for your child.

Oral Guided Reading When You Can't Give Your Child Your Undivided Attention

Ask your child to read out loud to you while you're doing a quiet chore in the house such as cooking, cleaning the kitchen, folding laundry, polishing your nails, or ironing (I used to ask my children to read to me while I sat on the floor stretching after a jog). You won't be able to pick up all her errors if you aren't looking directly at her book, but you'll catch some mistakes, and even this kind of practice will increase her ability to recognize words on sight.

Laughter and Lists

A relatively small number of words make up over half of the words children encounter in books (these are known as Dolch sight words, originally compiled by the educator Edward Dolch, Ph.D. in the 1930s and 1940s). If you help her practice reading such high-frequency words as *of, and, a, to, in, is, it, he, for, on,* and *are,* you will increase her ability to recognize them as whole words in a flash—and this automatic response will make reading easier and more fun for her.

Ask her teacher for a list of Dolch words or download them from the Internet. You can make up flash cards if you enjoy doing that sort of thing (which I don't—it's too much like work) or use the list of words for a game. You can challenge your child to a speed-reading contest and take turns reading individual words, columns of words, or whole pages to each other as quickly as you can. But be careful that you don't turn this into a boring drill. It should be a game.

My sons and I used to stretch out on the floor with the list of Dolch words between us and take turns reading columns of words out loud as fast as we could. Sometimes we'd set a clock or kitchen timer to see who could read the most words in a specific amount of time or who could improve the most on a second or third try. We'd try to outdo one another by reading faster and faster until we were so tongue-tied we were reading gibberish. By then we'd be laughing too hard to continue and the game would end. These practice sessions only lasted a few minutes, but they spruced up the boys' sight-reading ability, which was especially helpful to the two with dyslexia.

4. Minimize anxiety by being Dumbo's feather.

Remember the story of Dumbo, the little elephant with the big ears? He was afraid to fly until his friend gave him a "magic" feather that bolstered his self-confidence and enabled him to soar into the air.

Like Dumbo, your new reader may be anxious about her ability to fly across the page—especially if she knows there will be an important reading test at the end of the year, or if she is struggling with reading. Anxiety is one of your child's worst enemies. Reading involves both sides of the brain, and anxiety causes the release of chemicals that jam up the corpus callosum—the bundle of nerves that connects the two hemispheres of the brain—and prevent her mind from functioning efficiently. If she gets so nervous when she opens a book that she "blanks out," she may develop additional learning problems that will make it even more difficult for her to become a reader (it's similar to what happens to you when you're panicked about being late for an appointment and dash around the house searching for your car keys until you finally realize that you're holding them).

You can build your child's self-confidence and help her stay relaxed by "being Dumbo's feather"—that is, staying physically close to her while she's practicing. Your presence will be comforting even if you don't focus on her, and she will enjoy having you witness her hard work.

As often as you can, invite your child to "keep you company" by bringing her reading book to wherever you are in your house and reading to herself while you are doing your own quiet activity—reading the newspaper, paying bills, using the computer, knitting, doing yoga, nursing her baby sister. Or take your paraphernalia—book, bills, newspaper, knitting, computer, etc.—into her room and keep her company while she reads. This will make practicing a much less lonely, far more palatable experience for her.

By the way, being Dumbo's feather can also help your older child get started when she has to write a big paper or study for an important exam. Even the thought of starting can make your child so anxious that she can't concentrate. But if you go into her room and hang out for a while, your presence will help to calm her down, and she will relax enough to gather her thoughts. Once she starts working, you can exit the room and resume whatever it was you were doing earlier.

" *You can build your child's self-confidence and help her stay relaxed by 'being Dumbo's feather'—that is, staying physically close to her while she's practicing.*"

5. Reward! Reward! Reward!

It takes a lot of self-control for your child to practice reading day after day. So make a point of rewarding her for her efforts. Praise her for being responsible, diligent, hard working, and mature. Give her hugs and kisses. Express admiration for her perseverance. Make family-wide announcements about her sterling character. Give her toys and treats.

It is much more effective to reward a child for wonderful behavior than to punish her for lousy behavior. If you chastise your child or threaten to reduce privileges if she doesn't practice, you will create a toxic atmosphere in your home. This will damage your relationship and undercut your goal of associating books with pleasure in your child's mind.

Keep in mind that the word "discipline" comes from the same word root as the word "disciple," which is related to teaching, not punishing. To "discipline" your child means to teach her how to behave. By rewarding her for being diligent and praising her for being a hard working and responsible person, you will not only help her become a reader, you will foster traits that will enable her to create a satisfying life for herself as an adult. And don't forget you are also setting a pattern that she may follow later in life when she becomes a parent, an aunt, an uncle or an important adult in some child's life.

" It takes a lot of self-control for your child to practice reading. So make a point of rewarding her for trying hard to practice. Praise her for being responsible, diligent, hard working, and mature."

6. Create a Reading Nest.

Instead of banishing your child to her room to practice reading, ask her to choose a favorite place in your house and call it her Reading Nest. Give her a colorful pillow or fluffy blanket to snuggle up with when she's practicing. If she wants company while she's reading, she can bring her blanket or pillow to wherever you are in the house and set up a Portable Nest. Her temporary nest might be in her baby brother's room, on the floor next to your desk, on the living room sofa, or under the kitchen table.

One of my friends recently told me that when she ate dinner at my house for the first time many years ago, she felt something warm moving under the dining room table and assumed it was a dog or cat. But when she reached down to pet him, she realized it was one of my sons wrapped in a fuzzy blanket, reading while we ate dinner. My sons always enjoyed hearing the faint murmur of voices overhead while they were practicing reading. They said it made practicing more fun and much less lonely—and that extra practice ultimately helped them become skilled readers.

7. Stay flexible about practice sessions.

Teachers will suggest that you have your child read for thirty minutes every night. But there's nothing sacred about this number. Yes, the more your child practices, the more progress she will make. But if you're too rigid about practice sessions, she will feel trapped and resentful, and this will short-circuit your goal of raising an enthusiastic reader. Learning to read is more like a marathon than a sprint, and you don't want your child to burn out right at the beginning of the race. She will need years of practice to become an effortless reader, and no one session is all that important. Life is variable and so is your child. Adjust the length and frequency of practice sessions to suit her energy level, schedule, and mood.

Buy a kitchen timer or small alarm clock and call it her Reading Clock. When she sits down to practice, encourage her to set the timer for ten minutes, twenty minutes, or more, depending on how she feels. If she reads for ten minutes and the timer pings, encourage her to set it for another five or ten minutes. If she reads for a full thirty minutes, praise her for her hard work. If she's exhausted and is losing steam, tell her to quit and do a little extra reading over the weekend when she's peppier. She will truly appreciate your empathy and kindness and will forever associate reading with your loving and patient attitude.

> *Life is variable and so is your child. Adjust the length and frequency of practice sessions to suit her energy level, schedule, and mood."*

8. Dress for success.

I don't know about you, but when I'm wearing sneakers and sweat pants, I feel like exercising more than when I'm in a suit and dressy shoes. The fact that I'm wearing sporty clothes puts me in the mood to exercise and propels me to get out to the gym or onto the running track.

Similarly, you can help your child get into the mood to practice reading by encouraging her to create a special reading outfit. It can be anything she gets a kick out of wearing—a leftover Halloween costume, tattered tuxedo jacket from a flea market, favorite baseball cap, party shoes, or beloved T-shirt. Once she puts on her special reading duds, she'll have an easier time switching mental gears and shifting into practice mode.

9. Keep reading treats all over your house.

Fill your house with irresistible things to read—comic books, graphic novels, kid magazines, joke books, cartoon books, books about movie stars, animals, or sports heroes. Put enticing reading matter in your kitchen so your child develops the habit of reaching for a book or magazine while she's snacking. Leave baskets of magazines in your bathroom and frequently update your supply.

My children are adults now, but when they visit me, they still enjoy riffling through whatever reading matter I happen to have floating around in the kitchen while they have a snack. My kitchen shelf currently has a collection of Mark Twain's short stories, a picture book of cinema noir movie posters, a book on brain research, a gorgeous little picture book of Greek myths, two magazines, a detective novel, and some washable picture books for visiting toddlers. Keep these delicious reading snacks around the house—especially in your kitchen—and you will tempt readers of all ages to read for pleasure.

Chapter 6 Review

Main Points

- Reading is learned in stages, and each new stage is built upon skills learned at previous stages. The only way your child will be able to master new skills and progress to the next level of reading is by practicing at home every day.

- Your child is at a momentous crossroads: If she becomes an enthusiastic reader by the end of grade school, she is likely to view herself as a smart person, become an academic success, and have many personal and professional options in the future. But if she remains a weak reader, she may suffer a loss of self-esteem, become a poor or mediocre student, and have fewer choices in the future. Thus her life will spin off in a very different direction. It is important to note that learning to read is such a quiet process that you may not realize how vulnerable your child is right now—and how much she needs your loving support.

- Your goal is to make it as easy as possible for your child to get over the beginning stage of reading and develop enough skill to find pleasure in reading. Once this happens, she will read books for fun on a regular basis.

- Studies show that all types of children can become avid readers if they get adequate instruction in school and enough support and encouragement at home. If you believe your child will become a passionate reader, she will believe it too.

- If you continue to read aloud to her beyond first and second grade and she continues to enjoy books, she will want to become a strong reader and will be willing to put in the effort to attain that goal.

- Reading to a child who has already learned to read isn't "spoiling" or babying her. It is reinforcing the pleasure of reading, widening her vocabulary, and increasing her knowledge—all of which will help her become an expert reader.

- Guided reading is effective because a child needs to see a word at least three to four times before she can decipher it quickly and easily. When you give your child the chance to read the same sentences out loud several times, she becomes so familiar with those words that she can then recognize them in microseconds.

- Anxiety is one of your child's worst enemies. Your new reader may be insecure about her ability to fly across the page. You can build your child's self-confidence and help her stay relaxed by staying close to her while she's practicing. Your presence will be comforting even if you don't focus on her, and she will enjoy having you witness her hard work.

- It takes a lot of self-control for your child to practice reading, so make a point of rewarding her for her diligence.

- If you're too rigid about practice sessions, your child will feel trapped and resentful. You don't want your child to burn out. Adjust the length and frequency of practice sessions to suit her energy level, schedule, and mood.

• Keep your house full of fun, interesting things to read. This way, you can tempt readers of all ages to read for pleasure.

Actions

► Fuel your child's enthusiasm for reading by cheering her on. ("Rah, Rah!" not "Nag, Nag!")

► Make it as comfortable as possible for her to practice reading.

► Continue to read out loud through all the early grades.

► Ask your child to read out loud to you.

► Reward your child for practicing.

► Create a Reading Nest in a comfortable place in the house.

► Keep your child company while she reads.

► Don't be too rigid about reading practice sessions.

► Use a special timer as her Reading Clock and ask her to set it for ten or twenty minutes (or more). When the timer dings, encourage her to set it for another five or ten minutes.

► Have your child create a special reading outfit.

► Fill your house with irresistible things to read.

Chapter 7

Step Four ... continued: Give Extra Support to Your Struggling Reader

You—and only you—can prevent your child from suffering because of a reading problem.

You are your child's most important advocate, his greatest protector, his biggest cheerleader. No one knows him as well as you; no one can cushion his feelings like you; no one can save him from pain, humiliation, and frustration the way you can. Your support will keep him from feeling miserable about himself and will turn him into an upbeat, functional child in and out of school.

I'm fervent about this kind of proactive parenting because of my experiences as an English teacher and as the mother of dyslexic children. When I was teaching remedial English, many of my adult students told me that reading struggles in the early grades made school a hellish experience, made them feel like failures, and sent their lives careening off course. When two of my own children struggled to learn how to read, I gained an even deeper appreciation of how reading problems can have a far-reaching and sometimes devastating effect on children.

Reading is the first subject taught to children in school, and they tend to define themselves as being "smart" or "dumb" according to how well and quickly they learn to read. Most teachers try to protect students from embarrassment in the classroom by giving all levels of reading groups upbeat names like Stars, Sluggers, and Top Dogs. But children are very savvy creatures, and they always know exactly where they stand in relation to their classmates. If they have difficulty learning to read, their self-image can get damaged—and this can lead to a variety of emotional, social, and learning difficulties that can change the course of their lives.

Why Some Children Have Reading Difficulties

Literacy problems can be caused by a number of different factors: hearing impairment, physical immaturity, insufficient exposure to language during infancy and toddlerhood, emotional disturbances, ineffective classroom instruction, inappropriate reading programs, or dyslexia (which has to do with the kind of brain wiring a child inherits). The good news is that just about all reading problems can be corrected—and the earlier a problem is diagnosed, the easier it is to correct.

Note that there is a wide span of ages when children are physiologically ready to learn to read. Some children are able to read at age four; others need until age seven or later. This makes it a bit tricky when you're trying to decide whether to take action about your child's situation. On the one hand, if you push your child to start to read too early, you can cause rather than prevent reading troubles. On the other hand, if you let a reading problem slide too long hoping that your child will "grow out of it," the dysfunction will become harder to correct.

Yet one thing is certain: If you notice that your child is having difficulties learning to talk or read, you need to consult with his teacher and possibly a trained reading specialist. Reading problems do not vanish on their own. If ignored, a small language glitch can snowball into a much larger and more complicated predicament that will cause your child unnecessary frustration and humiliation. To borrow the famous line from Arthur Miller's play, *Death of a Salesman*, "...a terrible thing is happening to him.... Attention, attention must finally be paid...."

Dyslexia

Until the mid-1980s, experts could only conjecture about the causes of reading difficulties. But with the advent of new scientific diagnostic techniques, neuroscientists have learned that some children are born with the kind of brain wiring that makes it difficult to process language. Children who have the greatest amount of difficulty learning to read are said to be dyslexic.

Dyslexia has nothing to do with intelligence. In fact, dyslexics often have compensatory skills that make them brilliant and original thinkers (Leonardo da Vinci, Alexander Graham Bell, and Thomas Edison are just a few of the notable figures from history who were dyslexic). People with dyslexia are commonly skilled at visualizing a place or situation from multiple perspectives and excel in fields that don't require strong linguistic skills such as art, computer science, carpentry, architecture, math, sports, and music.

Some early signs of dyslexia are: having trouble learning to talk, learning the sounds of the alphabet, remembering the sequence of the alphabet, remembering words to frequently heard songs, memorizing facts, pronouncing words, learning a foreign language, and spelling. Dyslexia is an inherited trait, so if you or other family members had reading problems as children, keep a close eye on your child's development. But don't assume your young child is dyslexic because he can't write the alphabet perfectly. Not all dyslexics reverse letters such as *d* and *b*, as is commonly thought. Some dyslexics do not reverse letters at all, and many children who are not dyslexic do reverse letters when they first learn to write.

Whatever the cause of your child's struggle, he will benefit greatly from all the suggestions I make in **Chapter 6: "Support and Motivate Your New Reader"** (if you haven't yet read that chapter, read it now because it will help you understand why your support matters so much). If your child is struggling with reading, you will need to give him extra support in three ways:

1. **Make sure his teacher is knowledgeable about teaching reading and is using a well-designed, systematic reading program that has been scientifically proven to work.**

2. **Consult a trained, competent reading specialist as soon as possible.**

3. **Maximize your child's self-confidence and minimize his anxiety and embarrassment.**

A reading problem is not a life sentence. Research shows the human brain changes with experience. In fact, the new field of epigenetics has arisen from the concept that a person's environment affects the way inherited genes are expressed.

Advocate for Your Child in School

If you suspect that your toddler has a language problem, talk with his nursery school teacher and ask for her advice about correcting it as soon as possible.

If your child is in grade school and is having a hard time with reading, share your observations and concerns with his classroom teacher and the school reading specialist. Don't be accusatory or confrontational, but make it clear that you want to work with the school to solve your child's reading glitch before his self-esteem is damaged.

Tactfully ask the teacher whether she is using a science-based reading program that has been proven effective. Some school districts are woefully out of date and still use inadequate reading programs. In addition, since there is no one-size-fits-all learning blueprint, even an excellent program may not be the right one for your child. The truth is, most children can learn the basics of reading no matter what kind of program is used. But for a dyslexic child, an ineffective or inappropriate reading program can be a disaster. Studies show that many children who fall behind classmates in the early grades remain poor readers throughout their school years.

Inquire tactfully about the teacher's knowledge and experience teaching reading—and find out how she plans to solve your child's problem. Some teachers have not been well trained or have not kept up with recent breakthroughs in the field of reading, and a lack of knowledge and experience can translate into inadequate instruction for your child.

Alert the teacher about your child's sensitivities and ask her to do everything she can to cushion him from embarrassment in the classroom. Explore ways to help your child feel more comfortable so he'll be able to function well in school. For example, the teacher might be willing to give your child extra time to finish tests or in-class writing assignments, allow him to take exams on a computer, or modify or shorten homework assignments.

If the teacher isn't responsive or if you lack confidence in her ability to address the problem, make an appointment with a school administrator and ask her to get involved. The school is obligated by law to help you. The Individuals with Disabilities Education Act 2004 (IDEA), Section 504 of the Rehabilitation Act of 1973, and the Americans with Disabilities Act (ADA) define the rights of students with dyslexia and other specific learning disabilities. Children with reading problems are legally entitled to special services to help them overcome their handicaps.

If you don't feel confident that the teachers and reading professionals at your child's school will solve your child's problem, look for a trained reading specialist in your community. You can ask other parents for recommendations or get a list of professionals in your area from the International Dyslexia Association, a nonprofit organization dedicated to helping dyslexics, their families, and communities.

Reduce Anxiety and Build Confidence

There is a large emotional component to reading—and anxiety is your child's worst enemy. Chronic stress, which can arise out of reading anxiety, may impair his ability to sort out what's important, cause attention problems, and interfere with his short and long-term memory functions. If your child freezes when he opens a book, reading will become that much more difficult for him. The more relaxed he feels, the more efficiently his brain will operate and the easier it will be for him to make sense of words. So stay nearby when he's practicing and act as "Dumbo's feather." Give him a lot of verbal encouragement so he doesn't grow discouraged and suggest periodic breaks so his brain doesn't get overloaded.

It's important to let him know that there's nothing wrong with him and that he is intelligent and competent. If he is dyslexic, make it clear that his inherited brain wiring makes learning to read difficult but gives him advantages when it comes to three-dimensional activities and tasks. Even a young child can understand that everyone finds some skills easier to learn than others.

When he spends an inordinate amount of time on a reading or writing assignment and can't seem to finish it, either read the rest of the material to him or tell him to stop working on the paper and relax. Then write a note to the teacher explaining the situation so he doesn't get in trouble in school and ask the teacher if your child can hand in the work the following day or after the weekend. No one assignment is all that important. What is important is making sure your child doesn't become completely overwhelmed.

Express your confidence in him.

You need to tell him over and over again that you have absolute confidence in his intelligence, absolute confidence in his ability to learn to read, and absolute confidence that when he learns to read, he will enjoy it. Research shows that all children can become excellent readers. It sounds corny, but if your child knows you believe in him, he will believe in himself.

Explain that there is no timetable for becoming a reader.

Remind him that no one goes through life wearing a ribbon on his chest declaring how old he was when he learned to read. It doesn't matter when he learns to read. What matters is that he learns to read well enough to enjoy reading—end of story.

Accentuate the positive.

Constantly remind your child that though he may not be able to read as well as his classmates or siblings, he excels at other pursuits. Maybe he's an excellent basketball player, talented cartoonist, gifted gymnast, witty conversationalist. Like everyone else on the planet, he finds it easier to learn some skills than others. This is part of the human condition. Assure him that he will eventually catch up in reading and move on to new challenges in his life.

Shield him from embarrassment.

Your child may feel humiliated because he can only read beginner books although his friends are reading more sophisticated material. You can protect him from embarrassment when he has a sleepover or goes away to camp by encouraging him to take lots of cool things to read—comic books, graphic novels, collections of funny cartoons, or *Mad Magazine*. This will keep his ego intact and allow him to feel confident enough to read in a social setting.

Make sure teachers are using a suitable style of teaching for your child.

Children have different learning styles. Visual learners learn best by seeing; auditory learners learn best by listening; kinesthetic learners learn by doing and feeling. Make sure that the professional who is working with your child is using a method that matches your child's particular needs. If your child isn't making progress, you might want ask the teacher to try a different approach—or find a different teacher.

Guided oral reading is enormously helpful.

The ability to recognize and comprehend words instantly is the key to becoming an excellent reader. Although some children can learn to read a word by seeing it three or four times, your child may need to see a word many times before he will be able to recognize it effortlessly.

Guided oral reading (which I describe in detail in Chapter 6) is especially effective when it comes to developing automatic recognition. As often as you can, ask your child to read a short poem or paragraph out loud to you several times and correct his mistakes as he goes along. If he keeps losing his place, give him a ruler or index card to hold beneath the line he's reading so his eyes will track across the page.

I remember sitting with one of my dyslexic children when he was just beginning to sound out words. I was correcting his pronunciation of the *th* sound in the word "the." He said "ta" and I repeated "*th*-a." Then we turned the page and again he pronounced the word "the" as "*ta*." I realized that his brain still couldn't connect the letters *t-h-e* with the *th*-a sound. But by practicing reading, he eventually developed the ability to recognize that word quickly—and that made reading easier for him.

Encourage your child to listen to stories and books.

Reading aloud is an excellent way to keep your struggling reader enthusiastic about reading, increase his functional brain wiring, and widen his vocabulary. But you can also help him by encouraging him to listen to stories and books on CDs when you don't have time to read to him. The more words he listens to and processes, the easier it will be for him to learn to read.

You can get audiobooks at your public library or local book store, rent them through online sources, or go to the website for Learning Ally (http://www.learningally.org). Learning Ally (formerly known as Recordings for the Blind and Dyslexic) is a national nonprofit organization that provides a wide range of books and other reading matter for people who have difficulty reading because of visual, physical, or perceptual disabilities.

Play the Spice-Up-the-Book game.

If your child is reading a boring or repetitive book, suggest that the two of you "spice it up" by changing a few words (though remember: only write in books you own. Never deface a library or schoolbook!). This will allow your child to taste the joy of self-expression and have some fun being inventive and irreverent.

I invented the Spice-Up-the-Book game one night when my then nine-year-old dyslexic son seemed particularly discouraged. Most of his pals were already reading chapter books, but he was forced to slog through simple, often annoyingly predictable primers. To raise his spirits, I suggested that we "spice up" the rather boring book he was reading by changing a few key words on each page.

Subversive writing is a great release for children. Who are the literary characters they love to read about? Alice in Wonderland who gets bored with her sister and follows the White Rabbit down a rabbit hole; mischievous Huck Finn and Tom Sawyer; naughty Peter Rabbit who ignores his mother's advice about Mr. McGregor's garden; very naughty Peter Pan who won't grow up. Encouraging your child to play with written words this way will give him a chance to let off steam and have some fun while he's practicing a variety of literacy skills.

I kicked off the Spice-Up-the-Book game by crossing out some tedious words in the first sentence and making interesting substitutes. Then I asked my son to make changes in the next sentence. We took turns as we worked our way through the whole book, but he was editor-in-chief, so he always had the final say. Below is a sample of the original text followed by our "improved" version.

Original version:

*"Charlotte was a well behaved little girl. She slept in her
own bed at night and did not wake her parents up. In
the morning, she brushed her teeth, combed her hair, got
dressed, and cleaned her toys. Then she went downstairs to
have breakfast with her mother, father, and baby brother
David."*

Our "spiced-up" version:

"Charlotte was a ~~well behaved~~ horrible little ~~girl~~ brat. She
slept ~~in her own bed~~ on the floor at night and ~~did not~~ liked
to wake her creepy parents up. In the morning, she never
brushed her teeth, combed her green hair, got dressed, ~~and~~ or
cleaned her toys. ~~T~~When she went downstairs ~~to have breakfast
with~~ she said "Boo!" to scare her mother, father, and baby
brother David."

By the time we finished doctoring the book, my son was
laughing so hard that he rolled off the sofa and onto the
floor. After that first experience, we periodically spiced up
other humdrum children's books that we owned. In fact,
it became one of our favorite games. But that first book
remained his favorite. Twenty-five years later, I still have some
of these books on my bookshelf.

My Own Experience Raising Dyslexic Children

When my first son was born, my husband and I knew so little

about infants that I was surprised the hospital let us take him home. But one thing I did know: I wasn't going to let my infant son suffer because of the reading problems that had hobbled my former students. So I was ever mindful of the importance of language development in his new life. And, as I confessed in Chapter 3, *"Talk, Talk, Talk to Your Infant, Toddler, and School-Age Child,"* I was a bit bored when I had to spend hour after hour with him. So I talked a lot to my baby right from the get-go, mainly to entertain myself—but also because I had an inkling that it would help him to use language. My son turned out to be a calm, contemplative child who soaked up words like a thirsty sponge. When he entered first grade, he had no trouble learning the basics of reading.

So far, so good.

My second son, born four and a half years after his brother, was a different story from day one. Muscular, active, and prone to temper tantrums, he had little interest in learning the songs and ditties his older brother had rattled off as a toddler. Furthermore, though he was very bright, talkative, and charming, he paid no attention to the colorful letter and word posters that I'd hung on the walls of his room. When he entered first grade, he couldn't recite the whole alphabet, even though we'd recited it together many times, and he found reading a struggle.

On top of this, he seemed to have a problem processing spoken language. For example, if I asked him to do a few chores—put his drinking glass into the sink, shut the front door, and hand me a pair of scissors—he'd do one or two things, then insist I hadn't made another request. After he came home in tears a few times because his teacher accused him of not listening in class, I had his hearing checked. Nothing wrong with his ears, the doctor said. The problem seemed to be connected to his reading struggles.

I didn't understand why my intelligent little son couldn't read. In those days, even reading teachers didn't know much about dyslexia because the science of reading was in its infancy, and all sorts of oddball theories were still floating around. My sense was that for some physiological reason, my son's brain couldn't imprint the words and sounds he saw and heard. Since his school was academically demanding, I was concerned that his reading problem would damage his self-esteem and limit his ability to do his schoolwork. But I had a hunch that if he didn't become anxious about reading, received effective instruction in school, and had plenty of support at home, his brain would mature over time, and he would eventually become a successful reader.

What kind of "support" did I give him at home? Nothing esoteric or time consuming. I basically did what I had done with my first son—used words for fun in our everyday life. As far as I could, I also kept in touch with teachers to make sure his needs were being addressed in the classroom, and I monitored his progress in reading. I tried to keep his self-esteem high, his anxiety about reading low, and repeatedly told him that he would eventually learn to read well. I read aloud to him as often as I could and encouraged him to listen to audiotapes so he would continue to enjoy books. I played quickie word games with him as we walked down the street or sat in coffee shops so he'd be familiar with letters and words and would associate them with fun. I made it as easy as possible for him to practice reading and rewarded him for working hard at it by giving him words of praise, hugs, and gifts. I made sure his days included a balance of physical exercise, three-dimensional activities, and technology so he didn't become overly dependent on technology for entertainment. The result? By the end of sixth grade, he was an effective reader who always kept a book in the back pocket of his sports uniform in case he had some downtime during team practice.

Ditto for my third son, who needed even more time than his brother to become fluent. I knew he was in the clear at the end of seventh grade when he packed a copy of Julius Caesar's *The Gallic Wars* into his camp trunk because, as he explained, he hadn't finished it in class.

I'm sharing these stories to make the point that all kinds of children can become readers. I'm convinced that the biggest difference between my dyslexic sons and their classmates who did not become strong readers was that I knew it was possible for my sons to learn to read well—and I made it as easy as possible for them to achieve this over time.

You can do exactly the same thing with your struggling reader.

Chapter 7 Review

Main Points

- You—and only you—can prevent your child from suffering because of a reading problem. You are your child's most important advocate, his greatest protector, and his biggest cheerleader.

- If children have difficulty learning to read, their self-image can get mangled—and this can lead to a variety of emotional, social, and learning difficulties that can change the course of their lives.

- Reading problems can be caused by a number of different factors: hearing problems, physical immaturity, insufficient exposure to language during infancy and toddlerhood, emotional disturbances, ineffective classroom instruction, inappropriate reading programs, or dyslexia.

- Just about all reading problems can be solved—and the earlier a problem is diagnosed, the easier it is to correct.

- If ignored, a small language glitch can snowball into a much larger and more complicated problem that will cause your child unnecessary frustration and humiliation.

- Children who have the greatest amount of difficulty learning to read are said to be dyslexic. Some early signs of dyslexia are difficulty in talking, learning the sounds of the alphabet, remembering the sequence of the alphabet, remembering words to frequently heard songs, memorizing facts, pronouncing words, learning a foreign language, and spelling.

- A reading problem is not a life sentence, although it can become one if left unattended.

- Your child's school is obligated by law to help you. The Individuals with Disabilities Education Act 2004 (IDEA), Section 504 of the Rehabilitation Act of 1973, and the Americans with Disabilities Act (ADA) define the rights of students with dyslexia and other specific learning disabilities. Dyslexic children are legally entitled to special services and programs to help them overcome and accommodate their learning problems.

- There is a large emotional component to reading—and anxiety is your child's worst enemy. Chronic stress, which can arise out of reading anxiety, may impair his ability to sort out what's important, cause attention problems, and interfere with his short and long-term memory functions.

- No single assignment is all that important. What is important is making sure your child doesn't become overwhelmed and frustrated. If reading and writing become torturous experiences, he will stop trying to improve, end up feeling like a failure, and suffer serious consequences.

- Guided oral reading (described in Chapter 6) is enormously helpful to dyslexics.

Actions

▶ If you suspect your child has a language problem, talk to his teacher and ask for advice on how you can help to correct it as soon as possible.

▶ If your grade school child is struggling with reading, share your concerns with his teacher and the school reading specialist. Ask the teacher whether she is using a science-based reading program that has been proven effective.

▶ Alert the teacher about your child's sensitivities and ask her to do everything she can to cushion your child from embarrassment in the classroom.

▶ If the teacher isn't responsive, or if you lack confidence in her ability to correct the problem, make an appointment with a school administrator and ask her to get involved. Schools are legally required to help children with reading disabilities.

▶ If you don't feel confident that the teachers and reading professionals at your child's school will solve your child's problem, look for a trained reading specialist in your community and ask her to evaluate your child and help plan a strategy.

▶ Give your child a lot of verbal encouragement so he doesn't grow discouraged and suggest periodic breaks from reading sessions so his brain doesn't get overloaded.

▶ Let your child know that there's nothing "wrong" with him and that he is intelligent and competent.

▶ Remind your child that it doesn't matter when he learns to read; what matters is that he eventually learns to read well enough to enjoy reading—end of story.

▶ Protect him from embarrassment when he has a sleepover or goes away to camp by encouraging him to take lots of cool things to read—comic books, graphic novels, collections of funny cartoons, or *Mad Magazine.* This will keep his ego intact and allow him to feel confident enough to read in a social setting.

▶ As often as you can, ask your child to read a short poem or paragraph out loud to you several times and correct his mistakes as he goes along. If he keeps losing his place, give him a ruler or index card to hold beneath the line he's reading so his eyes will track across the page.

▶ Read exciting, amusing, fascinating material aloud and have your child listen to stories he likes on CDs.

▶ Play the Spice-Up-the-Book Game by changing words in a boring story to make it more fun.

Chapter 8

Step Five
Use—Don't Abuse—
Technology and Balance
Your Child's Diet of Fun

People often talk about technology as if it's a monster gobbling up children's desire to read. But then, tech bashing has been going on for thousands of years. The Greek philosopher Socrates complained that writing—the new technology of his day—would "create forgetfulness," that is, destroy memory and weaken the mind.

So let's get something straight: Digital technology is not an obstacle to raising a passionate reader. Admittedly, technology presents a challenge to parents and teachers. But even the jazziest, coolest, most up-to-date digital inventions are just machines—and like all machines, they can be beneficial or harmful depending on the way they are used.

Take any "old-fashioned" machine such as a hair dryer, washing machine, power drill, or automobile. Use it correctly and it will be helpful. Abuse or misuse it and it will be harmful—possibly even deadly.

The same principle holds true for newer inventions like TVs, computers, smartphones, tablets, and video games. If your child uses them well, they will be a big plus in her life. If she abuses and misuses them, they will be destructive and cause serious academic, emotional, and even health problems.

Therefore, your goal is to help your child use these machines in ways that will help rather than hurt her. How do you do this? By making sure there is a good balance of recreational activities in her daily life. Your child's day should include:

- Physical exercise.

- Play that involves real people and real objects in the real world.

- Technology.

If your child spends some time using digital entertainment and also gets plenty of physical exercise, interacts with people, reads books, and engages in spontaneous three-dimensional play, technology will have a positive effect on her. But if sitting and staring at screens is your child's only form of entertainment, her development will be stunted. As with many other temptations in life, moderation is the key.

How to Balance Your Child's Diet of Fun

The easiest way to balance your child's recreational diet is to approach it the same way you approach her diet of food. Let's look at how you deal with her eating habits.

Your child loves treats, sweets, chips, and fast food. But since you know her health will be compromised if she eats too many unhealthy foods, you've created a few strategies to prevent her from overdosing on them.

You began by learning something about nutrition so you'd know which foods are good and which are bad for her to eat. Based on this, you made flexible rules about what she can and cannot consume each day—and asked the other adults who care for her to abide by these rules. You limited the amount of junk food in your pantry and stocked up on fresh fruits, vegetables, and healthy snacks. When possible, you prepared nutritious snacks and meals. And you tried to be a positive role model by eating right yourself.

This is an imperfect system.

For one thing, you're not with your child all the time, so you can't always supervise her or keep track of what she eats. You don't always have time to prepare nutritious snacks and meals. You can't—or don't always want to—stop her from eating junk food at parties, blowout weekends, special events, vacations, movie theaters, etc. And you don't always set a perfect example for her. Sometimes you overdose on junk food, too.

Despite these challenges and lapses, you haven't stopped trying to keep your child healthy. You haven't announced, "It's impossible to feed my child nutritiously because healthy food can't compete with junk food," and then shut your kitchen. You haven't put a carton of candy and a soda machine in her room and allowed her to eat and drink anything she wants. Why? Because you are determined to keep her safe, healthy, and strong.

It's exactly the same when it comes to her diet of technology. If your child consumes technology in moderation, it will be beneficial. If she overdoses, it will cause physical, intellectual, academic, and social damage and narrow her future.

Positives and Negatives of Technology

The landscape of technology is changing so rapidly that scientists haven't had time to study the long-term effects of the most recently invented gadgets on children. But I want to run through some of the positives and negatives that are known about technology to give you an overview.

Television

Positives:

- TV is relaxing and entertaining for children.

- Educational shows (like *Sesame Street* or nature programs) can expose young children to new words and new information.

Negatives:

- Studies show that excessive TV use can cause attention and learning problems and classroom difficulties. Watching too much TV can reduce stimulation to the areas of the brain that are vital for development of language, reading, and analytic thinking; lessen mental "traffic" between the two sides of the brain; and diminish the development of parts of the brain that regulate attention, memory, organization, and motivation.

- Researchers have connected TV watching and weight gain, possibly because TV watchers get less exercise than other children and snack while they watch. As the number of hours children spend watching TV goes up, so do their body fat percentages.

- TV exposes children to hundreds of thousands of ads every year and makes them an easy target for exploitation. Toy and junk food manufacturers count on what they call "pester power" and the "nag factor" to sell products, and ads try to convince children that they need certain products to be cool, happy, and popular. This dynamic affects your child's self-esteem and your pocketbook.

- Some researchers believe constant exposure to violent shows can inure children to violence and make them less empathetic to other people's suffering.

Computers

Positives:

○ Children love using computers.

○ Computer skills are needed for success in our society. According to the Bureau of Labor Statistics Employment Projection in 2000, eight of the top ten fastest growing occupations were computer related, including jobs such as computer software engineer, database administrator, and desktop publisher—all of which require advanced computer skills.

○ The use of computers has broken down the barrier between school (which has been the traditional place of learning) and all other places, turning the whole world into a classroom. Children can now learn anytime, anywhere.

○ Computers can increase children's skills in art, math, deductive reasoning, and problem solving.

○ Computers provide a massive body of information and many different perspectives.

○ Some children find it easier to read on computers because they can change the size and font of the print.

○ Social media can allow children to create a wide social network.

Negatives:

○ Some psychologists and learning experts believe that the habit of hopscotching around the Internet to read short articles, postings on blogs, and social media has decreased children's ability to focus and concentrate when reading longer, more complex material.

○ Children can easily be misled by false or inaccurate information because they rarely check the credentials of web authors or go to additional articles on the same subject.

○ Young children are extremely vulnerable to commercial exploitation on the web because they often can't tell the difference between ads and unbiased factual information.

○ Children can be exposed to inappropriately sexual or violent material.

Video Games

Positives:

○ Video games harness children's passion for learning.

○ Video games help children learn that symbols have meaning—an important concept in our increasingly visual society.

○ Video games allow children to experiment with new roles in a risk-free environment.

○ Gaming offers immediate rewards for effort.

- Gaming success can build self-esteem.

- Playing games can speed up children's physical reaction time and increase their peripheral vision.

- Well-designed games can develop critical thinking and problem-solving skills.

- Games can enhance visual-spatial thinking—the ability to rotate objects in one's mind.

Negatives:

- The more time children spend playing video games, the less time they spend on homework.

- The fast pace of video games can lessen children's attention spans and make it difficult for them to focus on more complex tasks like reading.

- Excessive gaming has been associated with depression, obesity, and aggression.

- Recent research suggests that excessive gaming can interfere with a child's quality of sleep and her ability to remember vocabulary words.

Smartphones

Positives:

- Smartphones enable children to stay in touch with friends and help them create a satisfying social circle.

⊙ They give children an opportunity to express themselves emotionally while at a safe distance.

Negatives:

⊙ The constant flow of texts can interrupt children's concentration and interfere with their ability to focus attention on long-term projects. Multitasking has been shown to make people less—not more—efficient.

How to Help Your Child Get the Most Out of Technology

1. Think about the impact a new gadget will have on your child before you buy it.

Don't automatically buy a new piece of technology because it's the "hottest thing on the market" or because your child's friends already own the technology. Ask yourself whether it will enhance your child's life or become an unwanted distraction. Make sure all machines you purchase for your child are appropriate for someone her age. Decide where the machine will be located before you bring it home so it doesn't end up in your child's bedroom or in the kitchen where it will be a constant source of temptation. Filling your home with technology is like filling it with bowls of candy and chips. Less is more.

2. Stock up on supplies for free play.

Encourage free play by loading up on paper, pens and pencils, crayons and markers, scissors, glue, old magazines, maps, dolls, stuffed animals, or action figures. Use empty cardboard boxes as building blocks and encourage your child to play with kitchen items such as pots and pans, salad spinners, or plastic measuring cups. If a clock or radio breaks, ask your child to open it up to see what's inside. Fill a box with old clothes that can be used as costumes for pretend games. The more time your child spends playing with objects and people in the real world (as opposed to "virtual" digital play), the more her brain wiring will develop and the smarter she will become. Free play turns your child's whole body—not just her brain—into a vehicle for learning.

3. Make sensible rules about your child's use of technology.

Researchers have learned that parental rules about digital entertainment have a big impact on children's behavior. For example, in 2010, the Kaiser Family Foundation reported that American children spend approximately seven-and-a-half hours a day using technology. But when parents made any rules at all about the use of media, that number dropped by almost three hours a day. Yet less than one-third of children said their parents set any limits on their use of technology.

Tell your child why you want to limit her use of technology so your rules don't seem arbitrary or unfair (I used to tell my kids that if they stared at the TV screen too long their brains would turn to mush, and they'd turn into mushrooms).

Ask your child to help you come up with fair rules. Children are great at solving problems, and if the two of you negotiate an agreement, the rules will be more tolerable for her. She may balk at having limits set, but on some level, she'll appreciate your parental concern and care.

4. Do not let infants and toddlers watch TV or use computers.

Ignore all the hype about "educational" TV shows and computer programs for infants and toddlers. The most effective way for your child to learn how to talk, read, and think is by interacting with other people, not by watching TV, pressing buttons on a keyboard, or touching tablet screens.

A wide range of doctors, psychologists, learning experts, and brain researchers believe that exposing a child to computers too early can limit her cognitive development, have a negative effect on her health and social relationships, and possibly even damage her vision. Although scientists don't yet know the effect of fast-paced visuals, scary sounds, and startling images on infants and toddlers, their research suggests that parents of young children should proceed with caution. The American Medical Association recommends that TV viewing should be avoided for children under age two, and limited to two hours a day for children older than two.

If you do allow your infant or toddler to sit on your lap in front of a TV or computer screen, make sure you continue to talk to her while she's staring at the screen, and encourage her to talk to you about what she's watching. The more words that she hears, sees, and uses before she starts school, the more her brain wiring will develop in her language centers, and the easier it will be for her to learn to read.

5. Keep TV out of your child's bedroom.

Putting a TV in your child's bedroom and asking her not to turn it on is like installing a candy machine and asking her not to eat too many candy bars. The temptation is too great to resist—and in the end, she will suffer from overindulging in TV. Studies tell us that children with TVs in their bedrooms watch more TV and read less than other children; score lower on math, reading, and language arts tests; are more likely to have sleep and behavior problems; and have a higher risk of being obese and becoming smokers and drug users.

If you have a young child, keep the TV out of her bedroom and put it in a more public space where you and other adults in the house can monitor what she watches and how long she watches.

If your child already has a TV in her bedroom, try to figure out a diplomatic way to relocate it. If you storm into her room and remove it abruptly, you will start a war. Instead, tell your child you just learned that having a TV in her room could possibly harm her and ask her to help you find an acceptable alternate location in the house.

Give her time to adjust to the idea. Let her keep the TV in her room if she pledges to follow rules about its use—but make it clear that the privilege will end if she can't abide by the rules. Or install a monitoring device that will automatically shut the set off after a certain time period. Or offer her a reward for letting you remove the set. Maybe she'll be willing to give up the TV if you … allow her to stay up a half hour later every night? Install a basketball hoop on the driveway? Take her on a camping trip? Buy her a new bike? You could call this bribery, but I prefer to think of it as a reward for mature and cooperative behavior.

6. Do not keep the TV on all the time.

Studies show that the TV is kept on during meals in two-thirds of American households—and is kept on all the time in almost half of American households. Keeping the TV on is so common that you may assume it is innocuous behavior—a "normal" fact of modern life. But this practice will have a negative effect on your child's intellectual, social, and physical development—and prevent you from balancing her daily diet of recreational activities.

First of all, when you keep a TV on in your kitchen or dining room during meals, you link the consumption of food with the consumption of television, and send your child the subliminal message that watching TV is part of her daily diet.

TV continually bombards your child with advertising messages that do not have her health and well-being in mind. The average American child is exposed to more than forty thousand commercials a year, half of which are ads for soda and junk food. The less TV your child watches and hears, the less she will be brainwashed to eat junk food and buy trendy products.

Furthermore, by passively allowing the TV to stay on all the time, you allow the TV to be a "secret" parent who constantly dispenses advice about what is "cool" to eat, buy, and wear, and provides lessons on social and moral behavior.

Last, when the TV runs in the background all the time, it creates a constant distraction that can cause a condition researchers call "continuous partial attention." This condition will interfere with your child's ability to focus her attention on one single activity and will make her brain less functional and less efficient. Ultimately, this will affect your child's ability to learn and her success in school.

The less TV your child is exposed to, the better off she will be.

7. Physical exercise boosts brainpower.

Neuroscientists have recently discovered that exercise has a much bigger impact on the human brain than was formerly understood. Apparently, exercise jump-starts brain tissue into developing new neurons—and the neurons developed through exercise are extremely receptive to learning.

Since schools are cutting back on gym periods and recess time in order to provide more time for classwork, you need to be pro-active about keeping your child on the move. It doesn't matter whether she plays on organized sports teams, runs around in the park or your backyard, or gets exercise in her gym class. But she needs to get some exercise every day. The more physically active she is, the more her brain will grow and the smarter and healthier she will become.

8. Use technology with your child.

Sharing a tech experience with your child is a great way to have fun with her while building her intellectual and social skills. Make a point of watching TV or playing video games with her and talk about what you're doing and seeing. Ask her to teach you how to use a new tech gadget and help you practice on it. Playing while chatting about the activity are great ways to increase your child's exposure to words, give her new ideas to think about, communicate your values (which may run counter to the values promulgated by mass media), and strengthen your relationship.

9. Keep books and other reading matter in strategic locations in your home.

Keep enjoyable reading material in baskets and on shelves throughout your house—in bedrooms, the living room and family room, the kitchen, and bathrooms. If you fill your home with comic books, joke books, collections of cartoons, magazines, and novels, you will send your child the message that reading is a recreational activity—not something she just does in school. Don't be snobby about the content. Anything she enjoys looking at or reading is fine. If she loves comic books, load up on them. If she wants to read the same book over and over again, so be it. If she enjoys her baby sister or brother's picture books, excellent. The more she looks at books, the better she will become at reading.

10. Make sure your child has time to rest and daydream.

Resist the pressure to keep your child busy every minute of the day and encourage her to spend time lolling about in her room "doing nothing" or lying on her back outside staring at the clouds. She needs time away from technology and her friends to refuel and refresh her mind.

Interestingly, scientists have discovered specific regions of the brain they call the default network, which become active when the rest of the brain is inactive (for example, when we sleep). This part of the brain is able to come up with solutions to difficult problems that aren't available when the brain is busier.

Taking a break from stimulation during the day will allow your child's brain to absorb new material, transfer information from short-term to long-term memory, and come up with creative ideas and solutions to problems.

11. Be a positive role model.

Your child models her behavior on your behavior. You can't expect her to moderate her use of technology if you are glued to the TV; cruise the Internet for hours at a time; or talk, text, and check emails during meals. If you use technology judiciously and engage in other activities such as reading, socializing, and exercising, your child will behave similarly. The apple doesn't fall far from the tree.

12. Schedule minivacations from technology.

Plan a specific hour, day, or weekend when everyone in the family abstains from using technology. Make a point of using this time for nondigital activities and games: play cards and board games, draw or paint, build something, cook, read out loud. Plan a family vacation at a place that has limited digital distractions. Refrain from constantly taking photographs when you're outdoors and put your gadgets away to teach your child to look at the scenery. Even short breaks will remind your child that her own brain is a wonderful built-in supercomputer that she can use for entertainment.

Chapter 8 Review

Main Points

- Digital technology is not an obstacle to raising a passionate reader. Even the jazziest, coolest, most up-to-date digital inventions are just machines—and like all machines, they can be beneficial or harmful depending on the way they are used.

- Your goal is to help your child use these machines in ways that will help rather than harm her.

- If your child spends some time using digital entertainment and also gets plenty of physical exercise, interacts with people, reads books, and engages in spontaneous three-dimensional play, technology will have a positive impact on her. But if sitting and staring at screens is your child's only form of entertainment, her development will be limited. As with many other temptations in life, moderation is the key.

- Ignore all the hype about "educational" TV shows and computer programs for infants and toddlers. The most effective way for your child to learn to talk, read, and think is by interacting with real people—not by watching TV, pressing buttons on a keyboard, or touching tablet screens.

- Physical exercise boosts brainpower.

- Resist the pressure to keep your child busy every minute of the day and encourage her to spend time lolling about in her room "doing nothing" or lying on her back outside staring at the clouds. She needs time away from technology and friends to refuel and refresh her mind.

Actions

► Make sure your child's day includes a balance of physical exercise, play that involves people and objects in the real world, and technology.

► Think about the impact a new gadget will have on your child before you buy it.

► Stock up on supplies for free play: paper, pens and pencils, crayons and markers, scissors, glue, old magazines, maps, dolls, stuffed animals, or action figures.

► Make sensible rules about your child's use of technology. Ask your child to help you create rules that are fair.

► Do not let infants and toddlers watch TV or use computers.

► Keep TV out of your child's bedroom.

► Do not keep the TV on all the time.

► Encourage your child to get physical exercise.

► Use technology with your child. Talk with her about what

you're doing and seeing. Ask her to teach you how to use a
new tech gadget and help you practice on it.

▶ Keep books and other reading materials in strategic locations
in your home.

▶ Make sure your child has time to rest and daydream.

▶ Be a positive role model by using technology in moderation.

▶ Schedule minivacations from technology.

Chapter 9

A Final Word on a Passion for Reading

In this book, I have given you the tools to help your child become a passionate reader—someone who not only knows how to read but who loves to read. And, I am absolutely confident that you will be able to accomplish this goal for three basic reasons.

First, the fact that you have taken the time to read this book means you are aware of the importance of reading in your child's life and are determined to help him become a strong reader. Your engagement and positive attitude about reading will have a powerful effect on your child's lifelong reading habits.

In addition, Mother Nature has given you a big head start by endowing your child with billions of brain cells, a built-in drive to learn, and the capacity to develop language skills. These traits are part of your child's survival system. He is a highly motivated learner, a little learning machine. Now all you have to do is reinforce what comes naturally to him and you will be home free.

Third, no matter how busy you are, you can use The Five Steps I recommend in the course of your everyday life because they are easy and fun. Inwardly, I've always thought of my method as the "Ice Cream Cone Approach to Raising Readers." Why? Because, like an ice cream cone, my method has a simple design, is easy to grasp, appeals to all ages and types of people, can be flavored to individual taste, and revolves around pleasure.

And pleasure is a great motivator.

We have now reached the end of our journey together, but I hope this will be the beginning of a wonderful journey with your child.

Notes

For readers who would like to read further about the topics covered in this book, I have listed some of my sources, arranged by subject, as they appear in each chapter. Most of these materials are readily accessible via the Internet or local bookstores and public library systems.

INTRODUCTION: WHO I AM AND WHY I'VE WRITTEN THIS BOOK

Knowledge Gap Between Researchers and General Public:

Reading Rockets is a national multimedia project funded by a grant from the U.S. Department of Education and dedicated to "teaching kids to read and helping those who struggle." On the Reading Rockets website you can access a list of important federal reports on the best ways to teach reading:
http://www.readingrockets.org/research/federal/nichd2

Illiteracy and Aliteracy:

Fostering the Love of Reading: The Affective Domain in Reading Education, edited by Eugene H. Cramer and Marrietta Castle, International Reading Association, 1994. See page 4.

The Impact of Reading on a Child's Life:
Straight Talk about Reading: How Parents Can Make a Difference During the Early Years, Susan L. Hall and Louisa C. Moats, Contemporary Books, 1999. See pages 6–7.

Psychologist Daniel Goleman discusses the value of helping children develop social and emotional intelligence in his book, *Emotional Intelligence: Why It Can Matter More Than IQ.* Bantam Books, 1995.

CHAPTER 1: POWER TO THE PARENTS!

Parents Play a Key Role in Children's Literacy:
Ladders to Literacy: A Preschool Activity Book by Angela Notari-Syverson, Rollanda E. O'Connor, and Patricia F. Vadasy, Brookes Publishing, 1998. See Introduction.

Importance of Play in Children's Development:
"Play: Essential for All Children, A Position Paper of the Association for Childhood Education International," by Joan Packer Isenberg and Nancy Quisenberry, Association for Childhood Education International (ACEI), 2002: http://www.ci.pleasanton.ca.us/services/recreation/gb/gb-playessentials.html.

CHAPTER 2: IGNORE THE MYTHS ABOUT READING!

Myth: Reading books is a thing of the past in our technological society.

Education and Longevity:
"Longevity Up in U.S., but Education Creates Disparity, Study Says," Sabrina Tavernise, *New York Times*, April 3, 2012.

The Value of an Education:
In their book, *The Race between Education and Technology* (Harvard University Press, 2008), Claudia Goldin and Lawrence Katz explain that education remains a critical investment for success in life, especially the high school degree. They emphasize, however, that in the fast-developing economy of the twenty-first century, we live in a world of increasing specialization. A college degree on its own is "no longer the automatic ticket to success." See pages 325 and 352–53.

"Questions for Dr. Retail," David Brooks, *New York Times*, February 8, 2008.

Myth: Schools should teach children to read at an early age.

Goal Setting:
The Learning Child: Guidelines for Parents and Teachers, Dorothy H. Cohen, Schocken Books, 1988. See pages 174 and 186.

Detecting Dyslexia:
Overcoming Dyslexia, Sally Shaywitz, Vintage Books, 2005. See page 10.

Myth: Parents should leave the whole responsibility of reading to teachers.

The Parents' Role:
Becoming a Nation of Readers: The Report of the Commission on Reading, Richard C. Anderson, Elfrieda H. Hiebert, Judith A. Scott, and I. A. G. Wilkinson, National Institute of Education, Center for the Study of Reading, 1985. See page 57.

Testing:
In his *New York Times* essay "A Tyranny of Standardized Tests," May 28, 2000, Leon Botstein, President of Bard College, laments the increasing reliance on standardized testing in U.S. public schools at the expense of education for knowledge and understanding.

CHAPTER 3: TALK , TALK, TALK TO YOUR INFANT, TODDLER, AND SCHOOL-AGE CHILD

The Influence of Environment:
"Genes are servants of the environment," says Columbia University Professor and Nobel Laureate Eric Kandel, in his 2011 lecture at the City University of New York Graduate Center, "We Are What We Remember: Memory and

Biology." The lecture may be viewed at:
http://fora.tv/2011/03/28/We_Are_What_We_Remember_
Memory_and_Biology.

Elasticity of the Brain
Enriching the Brain: How to Maximize Every Learner's Potential, Eric Jensen, John Wiley & Sons, 2006. See page 1.

The More Words the Better:
The Social World of Children Learning to Talk, Betty Hart and Todd R. Risley, Brookes Publishing, 1999. See Preface.

Meaningful Differences in the Everyday Experience of Young American Children, Betty Hart and Todd R. Risley, Brookes Publishing, 1995. See pages 98–99.

You Have a Window of Opportunity

Early Stimulus:
Magic Trees of the Mind: How to Nurture Your Child's Intelligence, Creativity, and Healthy Emotions from Birth Through Adolescence, Marian Diamond and Janet Hopson, Plume, 1999. See page 2.

Acquired Knowledge and Reading:
Becoming a Nation of Readers: The Report of the Commission on Reading, Richard C. Anderson, Elfrieda H. Hiebert, Judith A. Scott, and I. A. G. Wilkinson, National Institute of Education, Center for the Study of Reading, 1985. See page 22.

Brain Wiring:

In this interview with David Boulton, Director of the Children of the Code Project, Paula Tallal, Professor of Neuroscience and Codirector of the Center for Molecular and Behavioral Neuroscience at Rutgers University and world-recognized authority on language-learning disabilities, explains what scientists mean when they say, "Neurons that fire together wire together": http://www.childrenofthecode.org/interviews/tallal.htm.

Easy Ways to Increase Your Child's Exposure to Words

Suggested Reading:

Games For Reading: Playful Ways to Help Your Child Read, Peggy Kaye, Pantheon, 1984.

Language Games to Play With Your Child, Allyssa Mc-Cabe, Fawcett Columbine, 1987.

Teach Your Child How to Think, Edward de Bono, Penguin Books, 1992.

125 Brain Games for Babies, Jackie Silberg, Gryphon House, 2012.

How to Talk So Kids Can Learn: At Home and In School, Adele Faber and Elaine Mazlish, Simon & Schuster, 1995.

Magic Trees of the Mind: How to Nurture Your Child's Intelligence, Creativity, and Healthy Emotions from Birth

Through Adolescence, Marian Diamond and Janet Hopson, Plume, 1999.

CHAPTER 4: ENCOURAGE FREE PLAY AND FIERCELY PROTECT FREE TIME

Executive Function:
"Can the Right Kinds of Play Teach Self-Control?" Paul Tough, *New York Times,* September 25, 2009.

Play and Physical Activity:
"Taking Play Seriously," Robin Marantz Henig, *New York Times,* February 17, 2008.

In their well-argued "call to action" article "Play: Essential for All Children, A Position Paper of the Association for Childhood Education International" (Association for Childhood Education International, 2002), Joan Packer Isenberg and Nancy Quisenberry demonstrate that childhood play is essential to proper brain development: "The recent explosion of research on the brain and learning delineate the importance of play." Their essay can be read online at: http://www.ci.pleasanton.ca.us/services/recreation/gb/ gb-playessentials.html.

"Why Play = Learning," Kathy Hirsh-Pasek and Roberta Michnick Golinkoff, Ph.D., *Encyclopedia on Early Childhood Development,* 2008: http://www.child-encyclopedia.com/documents/ Hirsh-Pasek-GolinkoffANGxp.pdf.

"Your Baby Is Smarter Than You Think," Alison Gopnik, *New York Times*, August 16, 2009.

Warning: Free Play Is Becoming Extinct

Play vs. Class Time:
"At Top Public Schools, the Arts Replace Recess," Kyle Spencer, *New York Times*, December 7, 2011.

"Playtime Is Over," David Elkind, Tufts University Professor Emeritus of Child Development, *New York Times*, March 26, 2010.

"The Fittest Brains," Gretchen Reynolds, *New York Times Magazine*, September 19, 2010.

In his insightful *New York Times* essay, "Let the Children Play (Some More)," (September 2, 2009), Stuart Brown, founder of the National Institute for Play and author of *Play: How It Shapes the Brain* (Avery, 2009) comments on the educational and social consequences of insufficient play for American children. He cites a University of Michigan study that charts a steep (50 percent) decline in unstructured play over the past twenty years.

Do Not Overschedule Your Child:
For more on natural play, see the above-referenced "Your Baby Is Smarter Than You Think," Alison Gopnik, *New York Times*, August 16, 2009.

Default Network:

In their article "The Brain's Default Network: Anatomy, Function, and Relevance to Disease," Randy L. Buckner, Jessica R. Andrews-Hanna, and Daniel L. Schacter explain that neuroscientists have recently discovered areas of the brain they call the default network. These areas only become active when we are not focused on the external environment—such as when we rest, daydream, or engage in an activity that requires little attention. During these periods, the default network goes into gear and acts to unravel complicated issues and solve problems. *Annals of the New York Academy of Sciences, The Year in Cognitive Neuroscience*, Volume 1124, March 2008. See pages 1–38.

Encourage Regular Physical Exercise:

In the above-referenced *New York Times* article, "The Fittest Brains" (September 19, 2010), Gretchen Reynolds writes about "the positive impact of even a small amount of aerobic activity" on brain development.

See also Gretchen Reynolds's "How Exercise Could Lead to a Better Brain," Gretchen Reynolds, *New York Times*, April 18, 2012.

***Give your child a few minutes of
undivided attention for play.***

Floortime:

Psychiatrist Stanley I. Greenspan invented an approach to teaching emotionally disturbed children that he called "floortime." Floortime consists of sitting on the floor with a child and engaging in some type of play that encourages him to interact and communicate. This type of play can help all children learn how to express their feelings, concentrate on an activity, develop the capacity for empathy, expand creativity, and learn new physical and intellectual skills. For further reading, see *The Essential Partnership*, Stanley Greenspan and Nancy Thorndike Greenspan, Viking Penguin, 1989.

CHAPTER 5: READ TO YOUR CHILD AND EXPAND HOW, WHEN, AND WHAT YOU READ ALOUD

Building Knowledge Early:
Straight Talk about Reading: How Parents Can Make a Difference During the Early Years, Susan L. Hall and Louisa C. Moats, Contemporary Books, 1999. See page 54.

Reading as "Fun":
How Children Learn, John Holt, Addison-Wesley, 1983. See page 150.

Reading Aloud:
Proust and the Squid: The Story and Science of the Reading Brain, Maryanne Wolf, Harper Perennial, 2007. See page 83.

How to Read to Your Child

Parent-Child Interaction and Reading as "Fun":
Beginning to Read: Thinking and Learning About Print,
Marilyn Jager Adams, MIT Press, 1990. See page 87.

Grover Whitehurst, Director of the Brown Center on
Education Policy at the Brookings Institution, is a
pioneer in children's literacy. He has written
extensively about what he calls "dialogic reading."
In his article, "Dialogic Reading: An Effective Way to
Read to Preschoolers," he states, "Children who have
been read to dialogically are substantially ahead of
children who have been read to traditionally on tests of
language development." The article is accessible online at
ReadingRockets.org:
http://www.readingrockets.org/article/400/

In this online interview with David Boulton, Director
of the Children of the Code Project, James Wendorf,
Executive Director of the National Center for Learning
Disabilities (NCLD), discusses dialogic reading as a way
parents and teachers can help increase reading
comprehension and vocabulary in children:
http://www.childrenofthecode.org/interviews/wendorf.
htm.

When to Read to Your Child:
*Endangered Minds: Why Children Don't Think and What
We Can Do about It*, Jane M. Healy, Simon & Schuster,
1990. See page 144.

Expand What You Read Aloud:
Proust and the Squid: The Story and Science of the Reading Brain, Maryanne Wolf, Harper Perennial, 2007. See page 123.

Educating Minds and Hearts: Social Emotional Learning and the Passage into Adolescence, Jonathan Cohen, Teachers College Press, 1999. See Chapter 1 for the history and importance of social emotional learning in education.

CHAPTER 6: SUPPORT AND MOTIVATE YOUR NEW READER

Warning: This Is a Critical Period in Your Child's Life

Parental Guidance and Attention:
Teaching with the Brain in Mind, Eric Jensen, Association for Supervision and Curriculum Development, 1998. See page 33.

Overcoming Dyslexia, Sally Shaywitz, Vintage Books, 2005. See page 234.

"Federal and State Strategies to Support Early Reading Achievement," Ebo Otuya and Susan Krupka, Educational Testing Service, January 1999. The authors state that a child's motivation to learn how to read is one of the factors that determine whether he will become a reader even if he finds reading a struggle.

Why Practicing Matters So Much in Reading

Brain Patterns and Reading:
For a description of the neural pathways associated with stages of reading, see page 78 of *Overcoming Dyslexia* by Sally Shaywitz, Vintage Books, 2005.

Automatic Recognition:
According to Maryanne Wolf, the importance of developing automatic recognition in reading cannot be overstated. See page 54 of *Proust and the Squid: The Story and Science of the Reading Brain*, Maryanne Wolf, Harper Perennial, 2007.

Marilyn Jager Adams, Beginning to Read: Thinking and Learning about Print—A Summary by Steven Stahl, Jean Osborn, and Fran Lehr, The Center for the Study of Reading, The Reading Research and Education Center, University of Illinois at Urbana-Champaign, 1990. See page 14.

The 2000 National Reading Panel Report—*Teaching Children to Read: An Evidence-Based Assessment of the Scientific Research Literature on Reading and Its Implications for Reading Instruction* describes the vital importance of automatic recognition. For nonfluent readers, "reading becomes a slow, labor-intensive process that only fitfully results in understanding." See Chapter 3 "Fluency," page 8. Published by the U.S. Department of Health and Human Services, the report can be accessed at:
http://www.nichd.nih.gov/publications/pubs/nrp/Pages/report.aspx.

Oral Guided Reading When You Can't Give Your Child Your Undivided Attention:

On page 235 of her book *Overcoming Dyslexia* (Vintage Books, 2005), Sally Shaywitz describes the importance of "reading and rereading aloud" with direct feedback from parents or teachers.

For more on the efficacy of repeated oral reading, see page 20 of Chapter 3, "Fluency," in the 2000 National Reading Panel Report—*Teaching Children to Read: An Evidence-Based Assessment of the Scientific Research Literature on Reading and Its Implications for Reading Instruction:* http://www.nichd.nih.gov/publications/pubs/nrp/Pages/report.aspx.

CHAPTER 7: GIVE EXTRA SUPPORT TO YOUR STRUGGLING READER

The Proactive Parent:

In an online interview at GreatSchools.org, Sally Shaywitz describes how a proactive parent can turn "an unhappy struggling reader into a happy, proficient one." To read this highly informative Q & A, "A Conversation with Sally Shaywitz, M.D., Author of *Overcoming Dyslexia*," visit GreatSchools.org at: http://www.greatschools.org/special-education/LD-ADHD/836-a-conversation-with-sally-shaywitz-m-d-author-of-overcoming-dyslexia.gs.

Self-Esteem:

In the above-referenced interview with David Boulton,

Director of the Children of the Code Project, Dr. Paula Tallal describes the intimate connection between language development, self-esteem, and success in school: http://www.childrenofthecode.org/interviews/tallal.htm.

Dyslexia:

In *Straight Talk about Reading: How Parents Can Make a Difference During the Early Years* (Contemporary Books, 1999), Susan L. Hall and Louisa C. Moats, describe how dyslexia prevents language learners from "recognizing, manipulating, and learning the speech sounds" that correlate to letters and words. See page 273.

Advocate for Your Child in School:

Hall and Moats are also strong advocates for early intervention if your child needs help learning to read. See page 155 of *Straight Talk about Reading.*

"Avoiding the Devastating Downward Spiral: The Evidence that Early Intervention Prevents Reading Failure," Joseph K. Torgesen, *American Educator,* Fall 2004: http://www.aft.org/newspubs/periodicals/ae/fall2004/ torgesen.cfm.

Beyond the Classroom: Why School Reform Has Failed and What Parents Need to Do, Laurence Steinberg, Simon & Schuster, 1996. See page 127.

Sally Shaywitz is also a proponent of helping struggling readers as early as possible: *Overcoming Dyslexia*, Vintage Books, 2005.

Encourage Your Child to Listen to Stories and Books:
Endangered Minds: Why Children Don't Think and What We Can Do about It, Jane M. Healy, Simon & Schuster, 1990. See page 144.

CHAPTER 8: USE—DON'T ABUSE—TECHNOLOGY AND BALANCE YOUR CHILD'S DIET OF FUN

In his article, "Mind Over Mass Media" (*New York Times,* June 11, 2010), Harvard psychology professor Steven Pinker advocates commonsense self-discipline, not outright rejection of technology.

Do Not Let Infants and Toddlers Watch TV or Use Computers:
In *Failure to Connect: How Computers Affect Our Children's Minds—for Better and Worse* (Simon & Schuster, 1998), Jane M. Healy writes that the "artificially engaging stimulus" of computers can inhibit natural brain development in preschoolers. See page 242.

In her article "What Role Should Technology Play in Young Children's Learning?" (*Young Children* 54/6, 1999, a publication of the National Association for the Education of Young Children, pages 26–31), Susan W. Haugland, a child development expert and professor emeritus of Southeast Missouri State University, warns parents against computer play for children younger than age three.

Alliance for Childhood is a nonprofit research and

advocacy organization of educators, physicians, and psychologists dedicated to promoting "policies and practices that support children's healthy development, love of learning, and joy in living." In their report *Fool's Gold: A Critical Look at Computers in Childhood* (Colleen Cordes and Edward Miller, eds., 2000), the Alliance advises that computers can have damaging consequences for children under age seven in terms of their health, social relationships, and intellectual development. To read the report or order a copy, visit Alliance for Childhood at: http://www.allianceforchildhood.org/fools_gold.

Acknowledgments

Raising Passionate Readers was written over a long period of time with the assistance of many people.

First, I want to thank my parents, Sydell and David Newman, for sharing their passion for reading with my sister Barbara and me, and for providing us with a lifetime of delight in books and libraries.

I am grateful to my sons Benjamin, Justin, and Adam who, as children, helped me test my theories and, as adults, critiqued them. Their insights, wide-ranging contributions, and continued encouragement have meant more than I can express.

I am indebted to visionary educators Ellen Stein, Gardner P. Dunnan, and the late Frank Moretti, whose suggestion long ago that I share my approach to raising readers with the Dalton School community in Manhattan sparked the creation of this book.

Heartfelt thanks go to the family members, friends, and colleagues who patiently listened to me talk about the subject of reading during meals and walks through Central Park, attended my lectures, and shared their own parenting stories with me. I am enormously lucky to be surrounded by such a loving, loyal, generous, and talented group of people.

I want to thank Kristin McDonough, Director of the New York

Public Library's Science, Industry and Business Library; Mark Bartlett, Head Librarian of the New York Society Library; Donna Brodie, Executive Director of The Writers Room; and Karin Taylor at the Library of the General Society of Mechanics and Tradesmen for assisting with research and providing quiet work space over the years.

I am also grateful to the terrific team at Tribeca View Press whose skill and hard work helped me turn my dream into reality: Editor-in-Chief Adam N. Elga; Art Director Régis Zaleman; Editors Robin Lyon Hegg, Thomas S. Clemmons, Erin Clermont, and Theresa Liu; and Marketing Director Shifra Goldenberg.

Last, a special thank you to my husband Henry, whose love and unwavering support made this book possible.

Bibliography

Adams, Marilyn Jager, Steven A. Stahl, Jean Osborn, and Fran Lehr. *Beginning to Read: Thinking and Learning about Print—A Summary.* Champaign-Urbana: University of Illinois, Center for the Study of Reading, 1990.

Adams, Marilyn Jager. *Beginning to Read: Thinking and Learning about Print.* Cambridge, MA: MIT Press, 1990.

Bauerlein, Mark. *The Dumbest Generation: How the Digital Age Stupefies Young Americans and Jeopardizes Our Future.* New York: Penguin, 2009.

Bender, Lauretta. "Specific Reading Disability as a Maturational Lag." *Bulletin of the Orton Society,* 8 (May 1957).

Bettelheim, Bruno. *A Good Enough Parent: A Book on Child-Rearing.* New York: Alfred A. Knopf, 1987.

Bettelheim, Bruno and Karen Zelan. *On Learning to Read: The Child's Fascination with Meaning.* New York: Alfred A. Knopf, 1982.

Bilton, Nick. "Resolving to Practice Some iPhone Abstinence." *New York Times,* Jan. 2, 2012.

Botstein, Leon. "A Tyranny of Standardized Tests." *New York Times*, May 28, 2000.

Bransford, John D., Ann L. Brown, and Rodney R. Cocking, eds. *How People Learn: Brain, Mind, Experience, and School.* Washington, DC: National Research Council Committee on Developments in the Science of Learning, National Academy Press, 2000.

Bronson, Po, and Ashley Merryman. *NurtureShock: New Thinking about Children.* New York: Hachette Book Group, 2009.

Brooks, David. "Questions For Dr. Retail." *New York Times*, February 8, 2008.

Brown, Stuart. "Let the Children Play (Some More)." *New York Times*, September 2, 2009.

Bruner, Jerome. *The Process of Education.* Cambridge, MA: Harvard University Press, 1960.

Buckner, Randy L., Jessica R. Andrews-Hanna, and Daniel L. Schacter. "The Brain's Default Network: Anatomy, Function, and Relevance to Disease." *Annals of the New York Academy of Sciences, The Year in Cognitive Neuroscience*, 1124 (March 2008).

Burrough, Bryan. "When You Text Till You Drop." Review of *iDisorder* by Larry D. Rosen. *New York Times Book Review*, May 12, 2012.

Chall, Jeanne. *The Academic Achievement Challenge: What Really Works in the Classroom?* New York: Guilford Press, 2002.

Cicci, Regina. *What's Wrong With Me?: Learning Disabilities at Home and School.* Baltimore: York Press, 1995.

Cohen, Dorothy H. *The Learning Child: Guidelines for Parents and Teachers.* New York: Schocken Books, 1988.

Cohen, Jonathan. *Educating Minds and Hearts: Social Emotional Learning and the Passage into Adolescence.* Teachers College Press and the Association for Supervision and Curriculum Development, 1999.

Cohen, Lawrence J. *Playful Parenting: An Exciting New Approach to Raising Children That Will Help You Nurture Close Connections, Solve Behavior Problems, Encourage Confidence.* New York: Ballantine Books, 2001.

Corbett, Sara. "Games Theory." *New York Times Magazine,* September 19, 2010.

Cordes, Colleen, and Edward Miller, eds. *Fool's Gold: A Critical Look at Computers in Childhood.* Alliance for Childhood, http://www.allianceforchildhood.org/fools_gold.

Cramer, Eugene H., and Marrietta Castle, eds. *Fostering the Love of Reading: The Affective Domain in Reading Education.* Newark: International Reading Association, 1994.

Davis, Ronald D. *The Gift of Dyslexia: Why Some of the Smartest People Can't Read ... and How They Can Learn.* Burlingame: Ability Workshop Press, 1994.

de Bono, Edward. *Teach Your Child How to Think.* New York: Penguin Books, 1992.

DeFord, Susan. "High Tech for the Disabled." *Washington Post*, July 28, 1998.

Diamond, Marion, and Janet Hopson. *Magic Trees of the Mind: How to Nurture Your Child's Intelligence, Creativity, and Healthy Emotions from Birth Through Adolescence*. New York: Plume, 1999.

Doidge, Norman. *The Brain That Changes Itself: Stories of Personal Triumph from the Frontiers of Brain Science*. New York: Penguin Group, 2007.

Duane, Drake D. and David B. Gray, eds. *The Reading Brain: The Biological Basis of Dyslexia*. Parkton, MD: York Press, 1991.

Duhigg, Charles. *The Power of Habit: Why We Do What We Do in Life and Business*. New York: Random House, 2012.

Eide, Brock L., and Fernette F. Eide. *The Dyslexic Advantage: Unlocking the Hidden Potential of the Dyslexic Brain*. New York: Hudson Street Press, 2011.

Elias, Maurice J., Steven E. Tobias, and Brian S. Friedlander. *Emotionally Intelligent Parenting: How to Raise a Self-Disciplined, Responsible, Socially Skilled Child*. New York: Three Rivers Press, 1999.

Elkind, David. "Playtime Is Over." *New York Times*, March 26, 2010.

Elkind, David. *The Hurried Child: Growing Up Too Fast Too Soon*. New York: Addison-Wesley, 1988.

Eyre, Linda, and Richard Eyre. *Teaching Your Children Joy.* New York: Touchstone, 1994.

Faber, Adele, and Elaine Mazlish. *How to Talk So Kids Can Learn: At Home and In School.* New York: Simon & Schuster, 1995.

Fink, Rosalie P. "Literacy Development in Successful Men and Women with Dyslexia." *Annals of Dyslexia*, 48 (1998).

Flesch, Rudolf. *Why Johnny Can't Read: And What You Can Do about It.* New York: Harper and Row, 1955.

Foss, Ben. *The Dyslexia Empowerment Plan: A Blueprint for Renewing Your Child's Confidence and Love of Learning.* New York: Ballantine Books, 2013.

Fried, Robert L. *The Passionate Learner: How Teachers and Parents Can Help Children Reclaim the Joy of Discovery.* Boston: Beacon Press, 2001.

Galinsky, Ellen. *Mind in the Making: The Seven Essential Life Skills Every Child Needs.* New York: HarperCollins, 2010.

Gardner, Howard. *Frames of Mind: The Theory of Multiple Intelligences.* New York: Basic Books, 1983.

Gee, James Paul. *What Video Games Have to Teach Us about Learning and Literacy*, 2nd ed. New York: Palgrave Macmillan, 2007.

Gladwell, Malcolm. *Outliers: The Story of Success.* New York: Little, Brown and Company, 2008.

Gleik, James. *Faster: The Acceleration of Just about Everything.* New York: Pantheon Books, 1999.

Goldin, Claudia, and Lawrence F. Katz. *The Race between Education and Technology.* Cambridge, MA: Belknap Press of Harvard University Press, 2008.

Goldstein, Sam, and Nancy Mather. *Overcoming Underachieving: An Action Guide to Helping Your Child Succeed in School.* New York: John Wiley & Sons, 1998.

Goleman, Daniel. *Emotional Intelligence: Why It Can Matter More Than IQ.* New York: Bantam Books, 1995.

Golick, Margie. *Playing with Words.* Markham, ON: Pembroke, 1987.

Gopnik, Alison. "Your Baby Is Smarter Than You Think." *New York Times*, August 16, 2009.

Greene, Lawrence J. *Kids Who Underachieve: Strategies for Understanding and Parenting the Academically Troubled Child.* New York: Simon & Schuster, 1986.

Greenspan, Stanley, and Nancy Thorndike Greenspan. *The Essential Partnership: How Parents and Children Can Meet the Emotional Challenges of Infancy.* New York: Viking Penguin, 1989.

Hall, Susan L., and Louisa C. Moats, *Parenting a Struggling Reader: A Guide to Diagnosing and Finding Help for Your Child's Reading Difficulties.* New York: Broadway Books, 2002.

Hall, Susan L. and Louisa C. Moats. *Straight Talk about Reading: How Parents Can Make a Difference During the Early Years.* Chicago: Contemporary Books, 1999.

Harris, Angel L. *Kids Don't Want to Fail: Oppositional Culture and the Black-White Achievement Gap.* Cambridge: President and Fellows of Harvard College, 2011.

Hart, Betty, and Todd R. Risley. *Meaningful Differences in the Everyday Experience of Young American Children.* Baltimore: Brookes Publishing, 1995.

Hart, Betty and Todd R. Risley. *The Social World of Children Learning to Talk.* Baltimore: Brookes Publishing, 1999.

Haugland, Susan W. "What Role Should Technology Play in Young Children's Learning?" *Young Children*, 54 (1999).

Healy, Jane M. *Different Learners: Identifying, Preventing, and Treating Your Child's Learning Problems.* New York: Simon & Schuster, 2010.

Healy, Jane M. *Endangered Minds: Why Children Don't Think and What We Can Do about It.* New York: Simon & Schuster, 1990.

Healy, Jane M. *Failure to Connect: How Computers Affect Our Children's Minds—for Better or Worse.* New York: Simon & Schuster, 1998.

Healy, Jane M. *Your Child's Growing Mind: Brain Development and Learning from Birth to Adolescence.* New York: Doubleday, 1987.

Heckman, James J. *Giving Kids a Fair Chance (A Strategy That Works)*. Cambridge: MIT Press, 2013.

Henig, Robin Marantz. "Taking Play Seriously." *New York Times*, February 17, 2008.

Hirsh-Pasek, Kathy, and Roberta Michnick Golinkoff. "Why Play = Learning" *Encyclopedia on Early Childhood Development*, 2008.

Hochschild, Arlie Russell. *The Second Shift: Working Parents and the Revolution at Home*. New York: Avon, 1990.

Holt, John. *How Children Learn*, Rev. ed. Reading, PA: Addison-Wesley, 1983.

Holt, John. *Learning All the Time: How Small Children Begin to Read, Write, Count, and Investigate the World without Being Taught*. New York: Addison-Wesley, 1989.

Hornsby, Beve. *Overcoming Dyslexia: A Straightforward Guide for Families and Teachers*. New York: Arco Press, 1984.

Isenberg, Joan Packer, and Nancy Quisenberry. "Play: Essential for All Children, A Position Paper of the Association for Childhood Education International." Association for Childhood Education International (ACEI), http://www.ci.pleasanton.ca.us/services/recreation/gb/gb-playessentials.html.

Jackson, Maggie. *Distracted: The Erosion of Attention and the Coming Dark Age*. Amherst, MA: Prometheus Books, 2008.

Jacobson, Jennifer Richard, and Dottie Raymer. *How Is My Second Grader Doing in School?: What to Expect and How to Help.* New York: Simon & Schuster, 1998.

Jansky, Jeannette, and Katrina deHirsch. *Preventing Reading Failure: Prediction, Diagnosis, Intervention.* New York: Harper & Row, 1972.

Jensen, Eric. *Enriching the Brain: How to Maximize Every Learner's Potential.* San Francisco: John Wiley & Sons, 2006.

Jensen, Eric. *Teaching with the Brain In Mind.* Alexandria, VA: ASCD Press, 1998.

Jones, Claudia. *Parents Are Teachers, Too: Enriching Your Child's First Six Years.* Charlotte, VT: Williamson Publishing, 1988.

Kahneman, Daniel. *Thinking, Fast and Slow.* New York: Farrar, Straus and Giroux, 2011.

Kandel, Eric. "We Are What We Remember: Memory + Biology." http://fora.tv/2011/03/28/We_Are_What_We_Remember_Memory_and_Biology.

Kavanagh, James F., ed. *The Language Continuum: From Infancy to Literacy.* Parkton, MD: York Press, 1991.

Kaye, Peggy. *Games For Reading: Playful Ways to Help Your Child Read.* New York: Pantheon, 1984.

Keller, Bill. "The Twitter Trap." *New York Times Magazine,* May 22, 2011.

Kennedy-Moore, Eileen, and Mark S. Lowenthal. *Smart Parenting for Smart Kids: Nurturing Your Child's True Potential*. San Francisco: Jossey-Bass, 2011.

Kirp, David L. *The Sandbox Investment: The Preschool Movement and Kids-First Politics*. Cambridge: Harvard University Press, 2007.

Kotulak, Ronald. *Inside the Brain: Revolutionary Discoveries of How the Mind Works*. Kansas City, MO: Andrews McMeel Publishing, 1996.

Langer, Ellen J. *The Power of Mindful Learning*. Reading, PA: Perseus Books, 1997.

Leonard, Laurence B. *Children with Specific Language Impairment*. Cambridge, MA: MIT Press, 1997.

Leong, Che Kan, ed. *Annals of Dyslexia: An Interdisciplinary Journal of the International Dyslexia Association*, 52 (2002).

Leonhardt, Mary. *Keeping Kids Reading: How to Raise Avid Readers in the Video Age*. New York: Crown, 1996.

Lyons, Carol A. *Teaching Struggling Readers: How to Use Brain-based Research to Maximize Learning*. Portsmouth, NH: Heinemann, 2003.

Manguel, Alberto. *A History of Reading*. New York: Viking, 1996.

McCabe, Allyssa. *Language Games to Play With Your Child*. New York: Fawcett Columbine, 1987.

McGuiness, Diane. *Early Reading Instruction: What Science Really Tells Us about How to Teach Reading.* Cambridge: Bradford Books-MIT Press, 2004.

McGuiness, Diane. *Growing a Reader from Birth: Your Child's Path from Language to Literacy.* New York: W.W. Norton & Company, Inc., 2004.

McGuiness, Diane. *Why Our Children Can't Read And What We Can Do about It: A Scientific Revolution in Reading.* New York: Simon & Schuster, 1997.

Mooney, Jonathan, and David Cole. *Learning Outside the Lines: Two Ivy League Students with Learning Disabilities and ADHD Give You the Tools for Academic Success and Educational Revolution.* New York: Touchstone, 2000.

Muller, Eric. *While You're Waiting for the Food to Come: Experiments and Tricks That Can Be Done at a Restaurant, The Dining Room Table, or Wherever Food Is Served.* New York: Orchard Books, 1999.

Nader, Ralph. *Children First!: A Parent's Guide to Fighting Corporate Predators.* Washington, DC: Corporate Accountability Research Group, 1996.

National Institute of Child Health and Human Development, National Reading Panel. *Teaching Children to Read: An Evidence-Based Assessment of the Scientific Research Literature on Reading and Its Implications for Reading Instruction.* Rockville, MD: U.S. Dept. of Health and Human Services, 2000.

National Institute of Education, Commission on Reading. *Becoming a Nation of Readers: The Report of the Commission on Reading.* Washington, DC, 1985.

Nisbett, Richard E. *Intelligence and How to Get It: Why Schools and Cultures Count.* New York: W. W. Norton, 2009.

Notari-Syverson, Angela, Rollanda E. O'Connor, and Patricia F. Vadasy. *Ladders to Literacy: A Preschool Activity Book.* Baltimore: Brookes Publishing, 1998.

Osman, Betty B. *Learning Disabilities: A Family Affair.* New York: Warner Books, 1979.

Otuya, Ebo, and Susan Krupka. "Federal and State Strategies to Support Early Reading Achievement." Washington, DC: Educational Testing Service, Washington, DC: January 1999.

Pink, Daniel H. *A Whole New Mind: Why Right-Brainers Will Rule the Future.* New York: Penguin Group, 2005.

Pink, Daniel H. *Drive: The Surprising Truth about What Motivates Us.* New York: Penguin Books, 2009.

Pinker, Steven. "Mind Over Mass Media." *New York Times,* June 11, 2010.

Ravitch, Diane. *Reign of Error: The Hoax of the Privatization Movement and the Danger to America's Public Schools.* New York: Alfred A. Knopf, 2013.

Ravitch, Diane, *The Death and Life of the Great American School System: How Testing and Choices Are Undermining*

Education. New York: Basic Books, 2010.

Reynolds, Gretchen. "Jogging Your Brain." *New York Times Magazine*, April 22, 2012.

Reynolds, Gretchen. "The Fittest Brains." *New York Times*, September 19, 2010.

Rich, Motoko. "Literacy Debate: Online, R U Really Reading?" *New York Times*, July 27, 2008.

Richtel, Matt. "Achieving a Healthful Digital Diet." *New York Times*, November 21, 2010.

Richtel, Matt. "In Online Games, a Path to Young Consumers." *New York Times*, April 20, 2011.

Root, Betty. *Help Your Child Learn to Read*. London: Usborne, 1988.

Rosenfeld, Alvin, and Nicole Wise. *The Over-Scheduled Child: Avoiding the Hyper-Parenting Trap*. New York: St. Martin's Griffin, 2001.

Shaywitz, Sally. "A Conversation with Sally Shaywitz, M.D., Author of *Overcoming Dyslexia*." Great Schools, http://www.greatschools.org/special-education/LD-ADH-D/836-a-conversation-with-sally-shaywitz-m-d-author-of-overcoming-dyslexia.gs.

Shaywitz, Sally. *Overcoming Dyslexia: A New and Complete Science-Based Program for Reading Problems at Any Level*. New York: Vintage Books, 2005.

Siegel, Daniel J., and Tina Payne Bryson. *The Whole-Brained Child: 12 Revolutionary Strategies to Nurture Your Child's Developing Mind*. New York: Delacorte, 2011.

Silberg, Jackie. *125 Brain Games for Babies*. Beltsville: Gryphon House, 2012.

Simpson, Eileen. *Reversals: A Personal Account of Victory over Dyslexia*. New York: Houghton Mifflin, 1979.

Snow, Catherine E., M. Susan Burns, and Peg Griffin, eds. *Preventing Reading Difficulties in Young Children*. Washington, DC: National Research Council, National Academy Press, 1998.

Spencer, Kyle. "At Top Public Schools, The Arts Replace Recess." *New York Times*, Dec. 7, 2011.

Spock, Benjamin. *A Better World for Our Children: Rebuilding American Family Values*. Bethesda, MD: National Press Books, 1994.

Stanislas, Dehaene. *Reading in the Brain: The Science and Evolution of a Human Invention*. New York: Viking Penguin, 2009.

Steinberg, Laurence. *Beyond the Classroom: Why School Reform Has Failed and What Parents Need to Do*. New York: Simon & Schuster, 1996.

Stevens, Suzanne H. *The Learning-Disabled Child: Ways That Parents Can Help*. Winston-Salem: John F. Blair, 1980.

Steyer, James P., *The Other Parent: The Inside Story of the*

Media's Effect on Our Children. New York: Atria Books, 2003.

Stipek, Deborah, and Kathy Seal. *Motivated Minds: Raising Children to Love Learning.* New York: Henry Holt, 2001.

Stoll, Clifford. *Silicon Snake Oil: Second Thoughts on the Information Highway.* New York: Doubleday, 1995.

Stross, Randall. "Computers at Home: Educational Hope vs. Teenage Reality." *New York Times,* July 10, 2010.

Tallal, Paula. Interview with David Boulton. Children of the Code Project, http://www.childrenofthecode.org/interviews/tallal.htm.

Tavernise, Sabrina. "Longevity Up in U.S., but Education Creates Disparity, Study Says." *New York Times,* April 3, 2012.

Torgesen, Joseph K. "Avoiding the Devastating Downward Spiral: The Evidence that Early Intervention Prevents Reading Failure." *American Educator* (Fall 2004).

Torgesen, Joseph K. "Preventing Early Reading Failure." *American Educator* (Fall 2004).

Torgesen, Joseph K. "The Prevention of Reading Difficulties." *Journal of School Psychology,* 40 (2002).

Tough, Paul. "Can the Right Kinds of Play Teach Self-Control?" *New York Times,* Sept. 25, 2009.

Tough, Paul. *How Children Succeed: Grit, Curiosity, and the Hidden Power of Character.* New York: Houghton Mifflin Harcourt, 2012.

Trelease, Jim. *The Read-Aloud Handbook*, 6th ed. New York: Penguin Books, 2006.

Turkington, Carol, and Joseph R. Harris. *The A to Z of Learning Disabilities.* New York: Checkmark Books, 2006.

Vail, Priscilla L. *Smart Kids With School Problems: Things to Know and Ways to Help.* New York: Penguin, 1987.

Wasik, Bill, Jane Avrich, Steven Johnson, Ralph Koster, and Thomas de Zengotita. "Grand Theft Education: Literacy in the Age of Video Games." *Harper's Magazine*, September 2006.

Wayne, Teddy. "A Smartphone Future? But Not Yet." *New York Times*, March 25, 2012.

Wendorf, James. Interview with David Boulton. Children of the Code Project, http://www.childrenofthecode.org/interviews/wendorf.htm.

West, Thomas G. *In The Mind's Eye: Visual Thinkers, Gifted People with Dyslexia and Other Learning Difficulties, Computer Images and the Ironies of Creativity.* Amherst: Prometheus Books, 1997.

Whitehurst, Grover J. "Dialogic Reading: An Effective Way to Read to Preschoolers." Reading Rockets, http://www.readingrockets.org/article/400/.

Wiener, Harvey S. *Any Child Can Read Better: Developing Your Child's Reading Skills.* New York: Oxford University Press, 1990.

Winer, Laurie. "Born to Check Mail." Review of *Hamlet's Blackberry: A Practical Philosophy for Building a Good Life in the Digital Age* by William Powers. *New York Times Sunday Book Review,* July 18, 2010.

Wolf, Maryanne. *Proust and the Squid: The Story and Science of the Reading Brain.* New York: Harper Perennial, 2007.

Wood, David. *How Children Think and Learn: The Social Contexts of Cognitive Development.* Cambridge, UK: Blackwell Publishers, 1994.

Index

abstract ideas, 58
admiration, expressing, 78
advocacy for struggling readers, 143–144
Americans with Disabilities Act (ADA), 144
anxiety, 129–130, 145–150
audiobooks, 96–97, 148

balanced use of technology, 161–162
bike riding, process of learning, 120–121
brain development, 46–47
    associating reading with pleasure and, 115
    benefits of free time and play for, 68–69,
    77–78, 174
    how a child learns to read and, 116–118
    physical exercise and, 79
Bureau of Labor Statistics, 164

cell phones, 166–167
childproofing of homes, 75–76
computers, 164–165
confidence, 19–20, 129–130, 145–150
continuous partial attention, 172

descriptive details for painting word pictures,
56–57
Dolch, Edward, 128
dyslexia, 141–142, 150–153

early reading, 35–36
educational attainment, importance of, 34
effortless reading, 118–119
embarrassment, 147
exercise, physical, 79, 172

flexibility about reading practice, 132–133
free time and play, 67–68

benefits of, 68–69
    caregivers encouraging, 81–82
    challenge of nurturing, 72–75
    childproofing the home for, 75–76
    decreased opportunities for, 70–71
    in everyday life, 80
    everyday objects used in, 77
    expressing admiration for, 78
    goals in, 78–79
    how to encourage, 75–82
    nontech, 76, 168, 174
    outdoor, 79–80
    overscheduling preventing, 71, 77–78
    parents' undivided attention for, 80–81
    studying the child in, 69–72

games
    spice-up-the-book, 149–150
    video, 165–166
    writing, 62–64
goals, 78–79
guided oral reading, 125–126, 147–148

hanging up interesting pictures, 52–55
happiness, 78–79
Hart, Betty, 47
Hart-Risley Study, 47

Individuals with Disabilities Education Act
(IDEA), 144
inferences, 49, 88
interactive reading, 87–91
    pleasure in, 91–94

Kaiser Family Foundation, 168
Kidsinco, 127

Learning Ally, 148
learning styles, 147
letters and words used as toys, 58–60
letter writing, 64

motivation for reading. *See* support and motivation for reading
multitasking, 167
myths about reading, 31
   and roles of teachers and schools, 35–38
   and technology, 32–34
   and time, 38–39

narrating life in real time, 55–56
National Assessment of Educational Progress, 22
National Endowment for the Arts, 22
National Reading Panel, 125
National Right to Read Foundation, 22
Newman, Nancy
   on changing how students feel about reading, 16–17
   classroom approach used in the home, 20–22
   on early reading problems and anxiety of students, 17–19
   experience as a new teacher, 15–16
   experience with dyslexic children, 150–153
Newspapers, creating, 64
nontech play equipment, 76, 168

outdoor play, 79–80
outfits, reading, 133–134
overscheduling, 71, 77–78

painting word pictures, 56–57
parents
   as first reading teachers, 36
   leaving responsibility of reading to teachers, 36–38
   as positive technology role models, 174
   power in raising passionate readers, 179–180
   sharing words and talking with children, 45–64
   tools to teach reading in the home, 20–22
physical exercise, 79, 172
pictures, hanging up interesting, 52–55
play. *See* free time and play

pleasure in reading, 28, 91–94
poetry, 127

Reader's Theater, 126
reading. *See also* support and motivation
   early problems with and anxiety over, 16–19
   effortless, 118–119
   five simple steps to enhancing children's skills in, 26–28
   guided oral, 125–126, 147–148
   importance of, 25–26
   myths about, 31
   national statistics on, 22
   nests, 132
   outfits, 133–134
   pleasure of, 28, 91–94
   sight, 128
   taught at an early age, 35–36
   technology and, 32–34
   time for, 38–39
   window of opportunity in language development and, 51–52
reading aloud
   after child learns to read, 124–125
   benefits of, 85–86
   by children, 125–128
   effective and interactive, 87–91
   materials for, 99–101
   with multiple children, 102–105
   pleasure in, 91–94
   sharing work, hobbies, and passions with children through, 106–107
   time for, 94–98
Rehabilitation Act of 1973, 144
rewards for reading, 130–131
rhyming, 60–61
Risley, Todd, 47

scavenger hunts, 63
self-confidence, 19–20, 129–130, 145–150
self-control, 130–131
sight words, 128
smartphones, 166–167
songs, rhyming, 61
sounding out words, 48

Spice-up-the-book game, 149–150

struggling readers, 139–140. *See also* students

  advocating for, 143–144

  reasons for, 140–142

  reducing anxiety and building confidence in, 145–150

  spice-up-the-book game, 149–150

students. *See also* struggling readers

  dislike for reading, 16–17

  early reading problems and anxiety, 17–19

  learning styles, 147

  national statistics on, 22

  self-confidence, 19–20, 129–130, 145–150

  self-confidence with reading and writing, 19–20, 129–130

subversive writing, 149

support and motivation for reading, 113

  for all types of children, 122–123

  by asking child to read aloud to you, 125–128

  benefits of, 115–116

  by bolstering child's enthusiasm for reading, 123–124

  by continuing to read aloud even after child learns to read, 124–125

  by creating a reading nest, 132

  in critical time of child's life, 114

  by dressing for success, 133–134

  effortless reading and, 118–119

  familiar method of, 120–122

  and how a child learns to read, 116–118

  by keeping reading treats all over the house, 134

  by minimizing anxiety, 129–130

  by offering rewards, 130–131

  by staying flexible about practice sessions, 132–133

  steps in, 123–134

  for struggling readers, 139–153

talking to children. *See* words, sharing

teachers and schools

  myths about, 35–38

  parents leaving whole responsibility for reading to, 36–38

  reading instruction given by, 36

  student learning styles and, 147

  teaching reading at an early age, 35–36

  trying to instill love of reading in children, 38

technology, 32–34, 159–160

  being a positive role model regarding, 174

  choosing physical exercise over, 172

  considering the impact of, 167

  effect on free play, 70–71

  how to balance use of, 161–162

  how to get the most out of, 167–175

  infants and toddlers and unnecessary, 169–170

  keeping books and other reading material in strategic locations as alternative to, 173

  and keeping television out of child's room, 170–171

  minivacations from, 175

  positives and negatives of, 162–167

  reading aloud with, 96–97, 148

  sensible rules about use of, 168–169

  turning off, 171–172, 174

  used with the child, 173

television, 162–163, 170–172

theater scripts, 126–127

time for reading, 38–39

toys

  books as, 105

  everyday objects as, 77

  nontech, 76

  words and letters as, 58–60

video games, 165–166

words, sharing, 45

  by asking questions that encourage children to think and talk about abstract ideas, 58

  brain development and, 46–47

  by encouraging questions and explaining answers, 57

  by hanging up interesting pictures and chatting about them, 52–55

  by narrating life in real time, 55–56

  by playing short, simple writing games, 62–64

  by rhyming, 60–61

  role in learning to read, 47–51

by using colorful words and descriptive details
to paint word pictures, 56–57
by using letters and words as toys, 58–60
window of opportunity for, 51–52
writing
age and good, 103–104
games, 62–64
subversive, 149

About the Author

Nancy Newman is a teacher, writer, parenting educator, and popular lecturer who has spoken to thousands of parents, grandparents, and educators on her approach to raising readers. Since 1995, she has given talks in a variety of settings—including events at the New York Public Library, Barnes & Noble, YMHA, Citibank, and Colgate Palmolive Corporation—and at many schools in the New York metropolitan area. Newman completed her graduate studies in English literature at the City University of New York, and taught remedial English in junior and senior high schools in the Bronx, and at a community college in Staten Island. Her first novel, *Disturbing the Peace* (HarperCollins), was published in 2002. Newman resides with her family in New York City.